Friendly Advice for the Future of China

Friendly Advice for the Future of China

Suggestions for
Political, Educational, and Economic Reforms
To Survive 21st Century Global Competition

Otto Tien-Pok Xing

The Hermit Kingdom Press
Cheltenham * Seoul * Bangalore * Cebu

FRIENDLY ADVICE FOR THE FUTURE OF CHINA:
Suggestions for Political, Educational, and Economic
Reforms to Survive 21st Century Global Competition

Copyright © 2004 The Hermit Kingdom Press

ISBN 0-9723864-8-3

Library of Congress Control Number: 2004110455

Correspondence Address:
The Hermit Kingdom Press
3741 Walnut Street, Suite 407
Philadelphia, PA 19104
United States of America

http://www.TheHermitKingdomPress.com

For the People of China and All Ethnic Chinese People
around the World, including the United States of America

CONTENTS

"An inch of time is an inch of gold but you can't buy that inch of time with an inch of gold."

Chinese Proverb

INTRODUCTION

Responsibilities facing the People's Republic of China are many. What China does in terms of economics, social programs, and political policies can have a deep impact not only in China, but in Asia and beyond. In fact, I would go as far as to state that China's actions will shape the definitive direction of the world in the 21st Century.

There are several reasons why China has been entrusted with this inescapable responsibility. They can be identified as current trends in global economics, international relations, and cultural developments. As various human forces come together in a powerful mix enhanced by major events in human history, China stands with the yolk of defining the future. Even if China doesn't do anything, that in effect is doing something. China no longer can be ignored or its internal policies deemed as merely isolated in its own sphere.

There are possible scenarios that can result from China's actions in the next few years. Global economics will see a transition and depending on what China does the direction can go in one of few ways. (It is too simplistic to ask questions in terms merely of benefit to China. The question is far larger in scope.) The Chinese impact will result in the betterment of the human race collectively or compel a form of Great Depression for the world. Although these oppositions may seem extreme, there are plausible reasons to expect such possible outcomes. The greatest factor (and the most convincing reason) is the size of the Chinese market (and the number of its citizens).

Not only the area of global economics will be affected. Global politics and stability can be impacted in far reaching ways. China's inaction is action, and whatever policies China actively adopts will lead global political stream in one way or the other. Just as when China built a dam, Yalu River flooded and destroyed precious monuments, whichever policy, however positive, will affect someone adversely. The road China should take, if it were to be ethical, is to adopt a course of action that results in a maximum benefit for the most people. To suggest that a policy to benefit all is possible is inane and impractical.

Chinese social policies, unlike its economic and political ones, will not have a direct impact on the global condition. However, China's socio-cultural programs will have an indirect effect on the world through the channel of politics and economics. If we agree that cultural policies impact domestic economies and politics, then this is not hard to see. And whatever changes made in do-mestic economics and political programs in China will invariably affect the world.

This book, therefore, privileges this po-tential import of China. This book is not meant as a historical study of China's past, a political science book merely examining the current condition, or a book only to be shelved in academic libraries around the world. This book is purposely meant as a direct tribute to China and its top government officials, to help them in setting out their policies for the next few decades. The author recognizes that there are many intellectuals working in China in all of these areas, but stand on the basis that different, more creative input can be gifted for China's wise counsel. Although this book's primary purpose is as a handbook for China's top leadership, it is the desire of the author that other Chinese intellectuals, students, laity will read it and benefit from it. They, too, as members of China can aid in the effective implementation of the suggestions in this book.

As for non-Chinese nationals, this book can serve as an informative guide for understanding China's potential. Whether the top leadership adopts the policies suggested in this book or not, the analysis in the book remains an important guide to China's situation and potential in the 21st Century.

CHAPTER 1:

CURRENT SITUATION IN CHINA

The fact that China plays an important role in global politics comes as no surprise. China's population alone provides the consumption potential that would whet the appetites of any consumer driven, supply-and-demand Capitalist. For decades, Western Capitalists dreamed of opening up China's market for Western financial gain. There are several reasons for the attractiveness of the Chinese market besides its sheer size. China has a large middle class. This term may seem out of place in applying to a Communist government from the perspective of the traditional market economy model, but in light of the changes China implemented to enter global markets, this term is suited to describe the consumers in China. Furthermore, if we are to describe the middle class strictly in terms of consumption, China has a big middle class. Average salary in China far exceeds that of the former USSR. Each and every Chinese citizen has more disposable cash with which to purchase products that enter their market. For foreign companies the cash flow alone really matters in determining a foreign market's middle class.

China does have a big middle class even in a more Western sense of the term, which combines cash flow with education. As a neo-Confucian state with a veneer of Communism blanketing its populace, the core Confucian value of education has continued throughout the Communist China. Confucian societies emphasize rising on the social ladder through education. Reaching the middle class by education (a model in operation in the USA) corresponds uncannily to the social value of China. It is no surprise, therefore, that China has steadily exported Ph.D. students to Britain and the USA even during its reddest Communist days. Many of these Ph.D. students represent China's poor who attained a status in China through the Confucian-value of education. As a neo-Confucian state, the Chinese government organized its educated and gave them authority with concomitant remuneration. As China entered global markets, this educated class, which is relatively large in number, were used to run local governments, businesses, and social institutions. Just as the Confucian China was linked to the smallest, lowest unit through an intricate system, so was Communist China. Despite its blatant Communist, all-out Proletariat, emphasis, China actually never escaped being a tiered society in the same way America is, albeit according to the Confucian model rather than a Capitalist one. There isn't the great gap between the wealthiest and the poorest any more than in modern USA. The Chinese structure made the continued growth of the middle class possible, and the structure was well-suited to a smooth transition to a more market-friendly economy.

Interestingly enough, China is in such a position that the very entrance of foreign companies will fuel the general rise of the middle class across the board. This is an important point to emphasize. Not all countries will see a rise across the board as the result of entrance of foreign companies. India is a good example of how despite the entrance of international companies, the wealthy become wealthier, but the middle class really failed to materialize. Some attribute the loss of BJP party in the most recent India elections to the failure of the realization of the middle class as promised by the party in the last elections. India finds itself in a position where the middle class has to be created from scratch. It's a difficult feat which intellectuals and capable leaders of India will eventually achieve. But it is safe to say the consumption potential is not there yet. So, foreign companies will "off-shore" in India and "out-source" in India, but they won't have extensive programs to sell their goods in India. There just isn't a middle class to afford an iPod. So, India remains only a producer of western company goods, at least for now.

China is different. Although the Chinese middle class does not have the disposable cash to the tunes of America or Germany, it does have disposable income for basic electronic and other consumer products. Coupled with the fact that there are 1 billion people in China, this market ends up being the size of Europe's consumer market. That is a big market and will produce many billionaires in a relatively short time. If a one-dollar-profit-product is purchased by China's middle class you become a billionaire almost overnight. Given the homogeneity of the market with a standard language, culture, and concomitant values (which advertisers can tap into to make consumers commit), China stands as the single attractive, untouched virgin market of any worth in the world.

What makes the Chinese market more attractive for western companies is that the current Chinese government has taken an aggressive interest in opening up its consumer sector for global businesses. Any company in the good side of China will make billions of dollars each year from China alone. When you consider, you can make that kind of profit from let's say, toothpaste, for our purposes, you can see the market's power when in Europe you will have to sell 10 million Dell computers to reach the same profit margin in one year. Selling 10 million Dell computers in Europe in one year, as great as Dell is, is impossible. Selling one billion dollars worth of toothpaste in China in one year isn't.

If you translate this market potential into computers, you can see the market's real power. While it's impossible to sell 10 million Dell computers in Europe, it is not unfeasible to sell 10 million Dell computers in China in one year some time in the near future. As the average wage of Chinese consumers steadily rise, an average middle class consumer in China will have the purchase potential of an average European middle class very soon. I would predict in the next 10 years. If China allowed Dell the Chinese presence, Dell can double its worth every year – a feat that is not currently possible.

The sheer fact of consumer potential for company profit is astounding. But that is not the only measure of the power of the Chinese economy. China can dictate any platform. And Microsoft has shown what dictating platform means in terms of the mighty dollar.

The company that can dictate the platform can be worth billions in 10 years. Bill Gates went from a Harvard drop-out to world's richest man in less than 20 years. He did not have to work hard at the same level for 20 years. As soon as he set the platform, money just flowed in. Programs had to be built on the Microsoft platform, which dominate consumer PC's. Royalties for each use, techno-logical assistance, and company alliances provided astounding profits. As most consumers only wanted the Microsoft platform, Microsoft market do-minance became unquestioned. Every time Win-dows was updated, Microsoft was assured of average of hundreds of dollars flowing in from every PC owner for various software purchases and company agreements. Browsers, advertisements and such based on the Microsoft platform made Microsoft profitable.

Microsoft even benefited in the long-run from pirates as pirating helped its market domin-ance. The poor pirating Microsoft programs, in effect, served as free advertisement and cemented Microsoft dominance in sectors that are hard to reach. If India's poor did not distribute Microsoft aggressively, the Microsoft platform's pervasiveness in India would have been more difficult to achieve. Although Microsoft may not make a cent out of millions of pirated Microsoft programs in India, the fact that the market ran on Microsoft and consumers depended on Microsoft ensured that any official computer project in India could not be done without some connection to Microsoft.

Just as publishers send out free copies of their books (at their own cost of printing, shipping, researching for the addresses/contacts of people who may be interested and would be important, etc.), Microsoft would have had to spend its own funds and resources for marketing and publicity. But because pirated Microsoft programs virtually distributed themselves to people who would be using Microsoft programs for the long run, pirates actually saved Microsoft millions of dollars in market research and promotional distribution of its products. Time, money, and manpower were saved while market was opened most effectively. Establishing a platform ensures future survival of the company and market share and profits. Bill Gates understands this so he does not crack down on piracy as aggressively as he could in countries which are poor and not dominated by Microsoft. As they say in the USA, "You can't buy that kind of publicity."

China, with its established middle class, can dictate a market by its sheer number. And China understands this power. A good example is the decision by China to use Linux in all of its systems. This decision has ramifications. First of all, as a freeware, China and Chinese firms will not have to pay Microsoft for Windows permits. This alone will save China and its market a few million dollars and make them disposable cash for investment, research, marketing, and product improvement.

Second of all, China can become the leader in Linux based software. It will make profit among Chinese consumers. But profit taking will not be limited to the Chinese market. As discontent with Windows platform rises, Linux users will increase and look to good software based on Linux. China will be there to get trillions of pounds, Euros, dollars, etc. from global markets. Given the security issues of Microsoft, many companies and businesses are already aggressively switching over to Linux. So, not only will China benefit from their Linux consumer base, they will also benefit from *de facto* Linux-enforced platforms among governments and in other corporate sectors.

China's understanding of the value of a pervasive platform propels its economic advance globally. China convinced Korea and Japan to officially drop Microsoft and adopt Linux. In a few years, you won't find Microsoft in these countries as the predominant platform. Given that these three countries represent the computer industry's center, China's future power in the computer software market is undeniable.

China's platform policy in regards to Linux is only a small picture of its potential to reshape any market and any platform. In essence, China will dictate how software companies design their programs and may even directly set policies affecting computer scripting, compatibility, etc. And such economic power is not in the area of computer platform alone. The potential is endless.

As European courts continue to penalize Microsoft, China is ensured of its victory in European computer markets if it plays its cards well. If America stands by Microsoft, American companies will most likely suffer fallout damage from the shift in the computer platform, globally. Microsoft is wise and it is transitioning into game consoles and other technology as Gates & Co. see that their dominance in the computer software industry has a limited lifespan.

One can see China's decision regarding Linux as its direct coup-de-tat of the software market. Although it is not too easy to see how China will benefit financially from this coup in the short run, it is certain that with time it will acquire tremendous wealth and power that Microsoft enjoy.

It is important to recognize that China is self-aware of its economic place and potential. Miscalculating China's understanding of its own economic power will cost companies billions in future revenue. Some companies will certainly go extinct very quickly, and they will only realize too late.

The Linux program is not the only example that shows China being aware of its economic power and potential in the global market. Recent research in technology and aggressive push of space programs indicate China's desire to capture the technology sector *en masse*. To doubt that China can do it is foolhardy. Chinese Ph.D. students at

MIT and Cambridge may dress badly (by western standards) and speak English that is difficult to understand, but they are not dumb when it comes to their field of expertise. In fact, Chinese Ph.D. students at MIT and Cambridge are arguably the best researchers in their fields at their stage. This explains why many leading institutions in the West are having to hire Chinese nationals into their faculty when recent Ph.D.'s struggle to speak English.

Just imagine, hundreds of Ph.D.'s from MIT and Cambridge (and comparable schools) are flowing into China in a period of a few years. And if you count all the Ph.D. programs around the world, that is a staggering number. It does not take a degree in rocket science to know that China will easily capture dominance in scientific development and technology in the next 10 years. The sheer number of researchers from China cannot be matched by any Western country. Given that China is placing itself in a position to lead the technology sector in 10 years or so, it is not difficult to understand the potential profit that will make China one of the wealthiest nations in the world, if not the wealthiest. I predict that this will happen in a period of 10 years without a war.

China's economic power, therefore, relies on its intellectual force. It is true that there is a brain-drainage; many Chinese nationals sign up with foreign companies. However, the sheer number of Ph.D.'s in China makes the placement of the majority of them in the West difficult. Since many of them can't speak English fluently, many western companies are afraid to hire them. Often, western emphasis on company team-work precludes hiring Chinese foreigners.

As they say in America, "One's loss is another's gain." In this case, the one who gains is China. Where will a Chinese Ph.D. in nuclear physics go if he cannot get a job in England after his Ph.D.? He is too ignorant about America to apply for jobs in the USA, most probably. He knows his nuclear physics but he doesn't know his Western culture, etiquette, or society. He will go back to China. If he can't get a job with the government or a big firm in China, he will work for a 2nd rate or 3rd rate firm. But on account of his Cambridge Ph.D., the 2nd rate or the 3rd rate Chinese firm will quickly become first rate. This progress will ensure profitability of these companies. A good example of this is found in Korea.

Samsung and LG were Korean companies with a local presence. But now, they are global leaders with a presence in every country that uses computers and electronics. The fact that many Korean Cambridge and MIT Ph.D.'s returned home and worked for them was certainly a key factor in the Korean rise to power in computers and electronics. The same potential is there for China, now that China has fully entered the global market.

Having a consumer market, the ability to set the platform, and the brainpower to innovate and perfect are all factors pointing to China's economic dominance in 10 years. Just remember that the internet was created for the consumer only 20 years ago. Look at how dependent every company is on this technological innovation. It is certainly not unfeasible for China to capture global economy and dictate terms for the world in 10 years as internet allowed Microsoft and other internet-based companies to do in the last two decades.

But the potential may not be fulfilled if China does not take active steps to control its future destiny. To leave everything up to chance will be a great mistake. China must implement political, educational, economic reforms needed to gain market dominance and future viability in the global market.

CHAPTER 2:

CHINESE POLITICAL RESPONSIBILITY

China must not relinquish its political responsibility; for, it is crucial for their economic advancement. The question of whether politics and economics are linked is highlighted in the case of USA. American political decisions often have a direct impact on the market. The stock market sees immediate increase or decrease based on a political decision. It is not merely the stock market that shows the connection between politics and economics. American political decisions influence economic trade. If Germany does not approve America's Iraq policy, its companies are more likely to seek companies in other countries to fulfill their economic (such as business-to-business) need, if at all possible. Governments have long used economic sanctions (in one form or another) to register their political protest.

China must be sensitive to the relationship between politics and economics. Although its sheer market size will be favorable for China in spite of its bad political decisions, a sound political policy will maximize its market and profit margin. More countries will commit their economic resources along with political favors when China shifts its political policy.

Why do I talk in terms of shift? Before answering that question, I would like to point out that I am one of the few who support slow democratization of Chinese politics. I use the term democratization in the general way understood in the West – such as allowing greater citizen participation in the political process. However, slow democratization may not keep up with fast-paced economic development as China is propelled forward as an economic force not only in Asia but globally.

In light of current developments, China must undergo a more drastic shift in its political program. What shift am I referring to? China must shift its politics in these key areas: (1) religion; (2) ideas; and (3) structure.

By religion, I refer to China's traditional anti-religion policy in line with their commitment to Marxism and Stalinist Communism. Many Christian missionaries have been killed in China, and they are often under that threat even today. China must realize that their anti-Christian political stance is no longer viable as they deal with Christian nations. Embracing Christianity will help China's advancement as many in the west consider their Christian commitment as the most important, or at least one of the most important identity markers.

When I say, "embrace," I mean, "legislate favorably." China must pass high-profile laws and political decisions in favor of Christianity. Such a domestic policy will receive a positive attention in the west and will raise the Chinese profile. For example, China can legislate an open-door policy for Christianity. China can officially state that Christian missionaries are welcome in China. China can provide easier visas for clergy from the West. China can also make greater ties to church groups.

For instance, China can invite Vatican legates to Beijing. A type of political discussion with the Vatican will not only be an act of good will, it will also be welcomed by all Catholic countries. Just to name a few, France, Spain, Portugal, Italy, Poland, Brazil, Argentina, and Mexico will be more favorably inclined toward China if China invites Vatican legates to Beijing. Even if this may not have any concrete political impact right away, there will certainly be a long-term gain for China.

Beijing can also invite other church representatives, such as the head of the Anglican Union, Southern Baptists' top leadership who dominate the American religious landscape, Lutherans of Germany and Scandinavia, and Orthodox Christian leaders of Greece and Russia. It is crucial that Beijing actively takes a pro-Christian stance. Without such a pro-Christian policy, the Chinese government will never be fully embraced by Western countries. It will always be under suspicion and mistrust. Christianity unites countries far strongly than political ideology. A small gesture of good will toward Christianity will go a long way.

To highlight the impact of Christianity and politics, I point to Russia. Russia aggressively embraced Christianity in recent years. Russia even spent tax money in church building projects. Russia passed several pro-Christian legislations. These practices, fully supported by the Russian people, indicated to Western countries that they are fully friends. Christianity has been important in the west for 2000 years, and it will be important in the west for 2000 years longer at least. China will not be able to maximize its full potential apart from a radically pro-Christian position.

There are other things that China can do politically besides inviting church leaders to Beijing. China can adopt a type of Christianity-as-the-most-favored religion policy as the Roman Empire did nearly 2000 years ago.

China can encourage setting up of Christian churches in every major city. In terms of political advertisement, the Chinese government should make documentary films and invite western observers and Western Christian media to write about this shift in the Chinese policy. China has so far underestimated the role of Christians in the West. It will cost them if they continue to do so, especially if China wants to maximize its political and economic potential. Even from a purely utilitarian and functionalist perspective, a pro-Christianity policy will advance China's economic power. The good will of Western Christians may be essential to the Chinese survival in the global market.

An anti-Christian policy can be the Achilles' heel that eventually allows China's enemies to undo it as Japan has experienced. Every Christian in the world does not have warm-fuzzy feelings for Japan since it is less than 1% Christian. You can condemn this sentiment in the West, but it is not productive to condemn. It's important to understand and legislate to China's benefit. If Japan had a more pro-Christian policy, more explicitly stated and publicized, the West would not have discarded Tokyo so quickly and without much afterthought.

Besides adopting a more pro-Christian stance, China must also make policy shifts in terms of the way it controls flow of ideas. In the Chinese context, it may be understandable why ideas are fiercely controlled. After all, it's not easy governing one billion people. Economically, China has been strapped for cash in the past, so it had to use political control mechanisms to maintain stability.

However, times are changing. China is set to be a wealthy, if not the wealthiest, nation in the world (if it is not destroyed by its competition). As such, China can loosen its control over ideas. In fact, given the fact that China is evidently becoming a main part of the global market, it may be essential that China allows greater freedom of ideas. You cannot let western countries with their flexibility of ideas into your country and then require your citizens to be limited in their freedom to express.

In effect, you are limiting Chinese nationals from competing effectively in this setting as the Chinese are limited while no such limits exist for their western competitors. If Chinese nationals are to be able to compete effectively, they must be allowed to play in the same playing field under the same rules. Without this right, individual Chinese competitors will lose not from the lack of intelligence or ability, but because of the unfair controls set by their own government. If you add up the individual losses, it is not difficult to see that it will have a deep, adverse effect on China.

I would even go as far as to state that if China does not free up its strictures on ideas, China subjects itself to a *de facto* colonialism-type experience where western companies come in, plunder its resources, and make profits, while Chinese nationals are hindered from developing as entrepreneurs, independent economic agents, etc. China will have technical control, but it will be relegated to a puppet position of merely permitting money to flow out of China.

It is important for China to allow freedom of ideas within its own population, so that they will be free to explore and adjust to changing conditions. It is only by allowing such flexibility that China and its population can naturally adapt to the fundamental changes in Chinese society and economics currently being experienced. In essence, I am asking the Chinese government to have more faith in its citizens. Just like being able to adapt is crucial to the survival of the fittest, China must adapt by free flow of ideas and discussions. China today is different from China yesterday, which was protected from outside influences as well as competition. China of yesterday was a closed, isolated market. That is no longer the case.

In addition to allowing greater freedom of ideas, China must also work on its structure. By political structure, I refer to the fundamental ways in which government is ordered. I would like to point out first that the Chinese government is very good from the vantage point of survival. It has survived, and we can say it is thriving. I would argue that this was possible in the past because it chose to be outside of western influence and contact. There were less variables. Now, as China actively participates in the global market place, there are more variables. The future is less certain. China must be able to wade through possible scenarios and meet any potential needs that might rise. I would recommend a few ways for China to proceed.

China must work towards a more representative government. What do I mean by this? While many may think in terms of elections, what I mean is actually a bit different. Greater rights to individual voters can be good, but it is not necessarily the best for China right now. The West has 2000 years of history of democracy, and the democratic process is a distinctively Western product. As such, democracy characterizes Western philosophy fundamentally and undergirds Western society even to the lowest common denominator.

The East is different. Democratic values have not been a part of the Asian experience and history for long. The people in Asia do not fundamentally think in democratic terms. To impose a Western-type democracy actually can hurt Asia rather than help it. China has been good because while it adopted Marxism, which is a Western philosophy, China catered it to the Chinese experience. China needs to do the same with democratic values.

While in the long-term China may want to allow greater voting rights, China should immediately advance greater representation. By greater representation, I mean putting more people in power who are representatives of the vastness of China. Perhaps, more importantly, it is a matter of survival to put more diverse people in power who can represent China's interests on the global market place and international politics.

An example of what I mean is provided. There are several million Koreans in China who are Chinese nationals. Although 3 million Koreans may not be much, it would be to China's interest to put them in power positions. Why? Korea is a major economic force. Having Koreans of China in power will facilitate cooperation and economic progress. In the same vein of greater representation, I would recommend putting citizens closer to the Indian border in power. Effective use of resources can go a long way.

The strength of the representative principle is not fundamentally democratic (at least, in the utilitarian way I am using it). Ancient China effectively used the idea of representation to create stability and maintain its hegemony in Asia. At one point practically every Asian nation sent a legate to China every year, and this symbolized harmony in Asia and bound Asian countries in obligation and ensured peace. With China's historical experience with representation, it can effectively implement the idea of representation catered to the modern period.

Unfortunately, China has not earnestly started their work in this regard. Beijing's leadership is quite homogeneous, currently. Beijing is showing that it is not being effective in maximizing Hong Kong for its gain. This could turn tragic. Beijing must go back to its own history, pool its brain resources together, and find a way to create a representative government. It's probably easier to do in a non-election based system at the moment.

In fact, many American Baptists complain that the American government is filled with so-called elected officials who do not represent their interests as a majority. Many Americans complain of a meritocracy that governs America at the expense of the majority. There is a deep discontent. Many popular, grassroots political movements in the USA actually stand directly opposed to current USA policies, such as forbidding Christian prayers in schools.

The current trend in the USA against homosexual marriage can be seen as an example of the explosion of popular protest against a small segment of society that pushes its wishes at the expense of the majority. The reason that President Bush is so popular has to be understood in this context. President Bush's stated wish to ban homosexual marriage as a US constitutional amendment is winning over the working class. While the working class generally vote Democrat, most working class oppose homosexual marriage far more than the upper class. For some working class, their anti-homosexuality stance takes precedent over other values they may hold.

China has to be wise in the way it structures its representative government. Just as if Bush had nominated a homosexual to his top government position, he would have alienated the working class, Catholics, and evangelicals, there is a bad representative government.

It would not be inaccurate to say that the Conservative Party shot itself by taking a pro-homosexuality position. It alienated the Christian vote. It alienated discontented Labour Catholics who might have jumped on the Conservative bandwagon if they felt that the Conservatives represented some of their core values. Conservatives further alienated most of the British public, who may not be anti-homosexuality openly, but are privately.

It is safe to assume that at no given time in modern western history that the majority in any given nation is pro-homosexual. This holds true in a fascist government contexts as well as in democratic government contexts. The Communists were among the most rigorous to crack down on homosexuals. Putting questions of whether homosexual practices should be condoned or not aside, utilitarian arguments militate against placing homosexuals in the government in most cases.

China certainly would suffer problems internally if it placed openly homosexual individuals in government as the majority of China, as the majority of India and Pakistan (its neighbors) are anti-homosexual. But it will suffer international repercussions as well in light of internal trends in individual Western countries. It is important to distinguish between open discourse and deep-seated inner thought/ingrained ideas. In most western countries, popular opposition to homosexual marriage is gaining greater public force.

These are only a few of the suggestions that I have from a utilitarian perspective. In the context that China finds itself, it is most important to use a utilitarian model. Some people think that a utilitarian model is by nature unethical. But such a high-stand taking often turns out to be out of self-interest rather than for the common good. We must see governments for what they are.

A government (in any form) is the body politic that represents people who have a membership in it. As such, a government exists for the sake of existing and protecting/advancing its members. Their fulfillment of *être* is morality. If a government cannot look out for the interests of its majority, then it has failed morally or otherwise.

Since people are not objects but thinking individuals looking out for their own good, most people could tolerate a government that fundamentally sticks to this value of a government. But a government that sacrifices the majority merely for the whims of a few often ends up suffering extinction, as the French Revolution and the American Revolution showed. These events in history highlight that the utmost ethics and morality for a government are to survive intact as a government and represent the needs and the interest of the majority, even if sacrificing of the minority may be need to achieve the ethical goal.

In effect, when there is a majority at stake, a good government will sacrifice the minority to protect the majority. If it does not, that will be its undoing, as a government is the sum of the majority of its members and can only exist in the long run as such.

Chapter 3:

Chinese Educational System

Ancient Romans emphasized *paideia* as a foundation for its society. Romans believed that effective education is crucial to building a solid society that will last. Many Christians have even come to see the Roman emphasis on education as facilitating the spread of the Gospel. The Roman emphasis on education and culture highlights the availability of effective channels of communication to the lowest common denominator. Some even perceive the Holy Roman Empire of the Middle Ages as the direct descendant of (or a smooth transition from) the Roman Empire of the Late Antiquity. Thus, some would argue that without the progress on education by the Romans even the Christian Europe would not have realized greatness.

I mention the Romans to stress the importance of an effective educational program for China. China is no longer isolated in its own realm, and it must modify its educational programs to enable its citizens to understand their situation and to be able to participate effectively in the global community. Such a program and goals are crucial to China's national success since China is the sum of its citizens. Enabling all citizens to reach their full potential vis-à-vis the global community will be more and more important as China becomes more intricately tied to global markets and international politics.

I have a few suggestions for China as it considers its educational programs in the modern context. I will focus on these areas: (1) English; (2) Western Classics; and (3) Christianity.

Before tackling the areas that I have mentioned, I will explain why I did not include science and technology. The primary reason is that I know that China has already privileged its science and technology programs. This is evident from the Chinese push to advance its space program. Furthermore, China aggressively sends its best science students for doctoral research at world's best institutions. In fact, it would not be wrong to say that over 50 per cent of China's Ph.D. students in the West are in some kind of science and technology fields. As China has privileged its science programs, I do not feel that they need further encouragement in this area. I believe China will continue to do a good job and that China's science and technology program will continue to advance and even overtake most western countries in the next 20 years.

A problem that I see is that the Chinese emphasis on science and technology is causing denigrating of attention on other important fields. It is not difficult to see why China may have problems seeing non-science subjects as very important. What is the relevance of certain fields, particularly in the humanities and the arts, to the concerns of progress and technological innovation? It is easy to assume that it is important to focus all resources directly in gaining a technological edge. Especially in light of the seeming direct link between technological innovation and economic advantage, it appears important that limited resources be allocated to maximize scientific research.

While it is not difficult to see the rationale for scientific investment, I would argue that it would be foolhardy to ignore other disciplines. My argument hinges on several factors. First of all, overarching investment in the sciences goes against Chinese history and character as a people. China has invested heavily in humanistic research particularly in the ancient days. In fact, the Confucian form of government can be seen as based primarily on humanistic studies, and China's glory days were at a time when humanistic research reigned supreme.

This makes sense because the Confucian system emphasizes human relationships. Even nature and what would be relegated to the sciences of today were understood to be influenced by human relations. Surprisingly, such humanistic emphasis mirrors the Christian emphasis. Christianity emphasizes understanding human relationships and configures society and nature in terms of relationships – either relationship between God and humans or relationship between humans. With this philosophy, Christianity has compelled advancement in philosophy, theology, and historical research. Scientific study, such as astronomy, actually benefited as nature was seen as tied to relationships. So it's also in Confucianism where cosmic order and sciences are seen to be tied to relationships, and the emphasis on human relations has experienced advancements in scientific research.

China cannot ignore the fact that its glory days saw the greatest light when humanistic research received their greatest attention. Even from a practical perspective, this makes sense. People are people. People are bound to their associations. These associations have a bearing on their thinking, including the way they think about nature and the scientific world.

One good example that illustrates this point can be found in the movie, "A Beautiful Mind." The protagonist of the movie, representing a real-life Nobel Prize winner in Mathematics, is shown to have a thinker's block. He is a mathematician. His solutions are assumed to be mathematical equations. But all assumptions are proven wrong in the film. What actually solves the mathematical blockage for the Nobel Prize winner is not more equations, but a time spent in a bar. He is talking with his friends about the problem of competition in trying to "get laid." He explains that if all the guys go after a beautiful girl, the probability is that none will get laid, at least not from the same group of friends. Each guy from the group going after the girl will cancel each other out in the competition. Once the beautiful girl rejects them, they will not have a chance with her less beautiful friends in the group because no one likes to be second choice. So the Nobel Prize winner suggests that they ignore the beautiful girl and all go after her uglier friends. Then, they will all get laid. Using this experience, the Nobel Prize winner suggested a game theory that not only impacted mathematics and economics, but also politics and international relations.

This shows that the Confucian philosophy of human relationships holding keys to nature and the cosmos can certainly have applications in such fields as political science and international relations (and even economics and "scientific" fields). Had the movie protagonist not had that experience and talk of getting laid, he would not have solved his mathematical riddle and come up with a Nobel Prize winning mathematical formula.

This is only one example of the relevance of human relationships and the implications of humanistic research directly on scientific study. Thus, I would encourage China to look to its past and see the import of non-scientific studies for its future and goals.

My argument for privileging non-scientific disciplines also comes from the argument of practicality. While scientific knowledge and ad-vancement is important, often it is non-scientific factors that determine outcome.

In the last generation Japan did not gain dominance in auto and computer industry because they had the best researchers in science. In fact, America was far more advanced and was often the first to develop new technologies. Japan effectively copied America's findings and made them more market friendly. In fact, it was Japan's understand-ing of what the common man may be attracted to that made them billions and won them the market dominance. America had the greater technological know-how, but American companies were not able to market the new technologies effectively in terms of popular consumption. This cost America its dominance in the auto industry and electronics. It is safe to say that despite the fact that America is still the number one researcher in technology and science, they are certainly not the dominant player in the market.

China must learn their lessons from this. It is important to keep up with research, but in the information age such as today, it is not necessarily the most important that you first come up with a new find. The world will know what is out there fairly quickly through the internet and other channels. The more important factor is understanding people and what they want. A country which can do this effectively will be able to apply existing technology to gain market dominance. There is a reason why Korea with pennies invested in research compared to the USA boasts being the 2nd best in the world in semi-conductors. They effectively built on existing US research and learned to pinpoint in the area of need. It has risen to the 2nd place beating out countries with greater research funds and many more scientists. Understanding human experiences and relationships will allow better effective management of existent resources. Like a football team that may win or lose based on the way individual team member is arranged and directed, a company will rise or fall based on its effective use of resources at hand. A company can have top players but it won't necessarily win the World Cup since victory is always a combination of factors. China has to remember this and realize that a star science program will not ensure its market dominance or scientific leadership. Often, effective human resource management is more important than having leading scientists in terms of consequences for the market and a nation's economic progress.

It is in this spirit that I would like to highlight areas which the Chinese educational program must pay particular attention to. As mentioned before, they are (1) English; (2) Western classics; and (3) Christianity.

My argument for privileging teaching of English is simple. English is important because it is the *de facto* global language. This reality can be attributed to several factors. The fact that the internet has been developed in the USA made English central in programming and web-design. People of other nationalities quickly learned English to participate in the web revolution. Korea and Japan have effectively become participants as well as Germany and Scandinavia. Most web developers and programmers will know enough English to excel in their field. And many non-Americans now occupy a prominent – even leadership – role in the computer industry. It is safe to assert that they needed English to do this.

Another reason why English has become a global language is simply via use. As more and more countries used English, it became a practical tool for people of different cultures to communicate.

Whereas most likely a Korean does not know Hungarian and a Hungarian does not know Korean, it is more likely that they will know some English. Any communication, therefore, will have to be done in English.

Using English as a communication language is not merely on personal levels. Ironically enough, as European nations pushed for unity in the form of the European Union, they have become increasingly dependent on English as the language of communication. A part of the reason is tied to the fact that English is generally taught in every European country, particularly after the fall of the Soviet Union. But there is more to it than that. As increasingly diverse nations come together in the European Union, English becomes a language that is more or less neutral. Most importantly, as big countries, such as France and Germany, jockey for power, they find English as a neutral language through which they can chart their influence. Both Germany and France have a history of animosity in Europe. Their use of English in a European forum detracts from the past and provides them with new opportunities in the united Europe.

Some may argue that English is the official language of England and would give England a greater influence. But it is important to remember that England today is perceived by France and Germany as a non-factor. This may change in the future if the United Kingdom has a competent government as the one they had during the Victorian and Elizabethan eras, which can compete on global terms and win. But the current British government is proving to be an economic failure and a non-entity in Europe. As a non-threatening member of the European Union, no major European country is particularly worried about using English as a *de facto* official language of the European Union.

I have mentioned before that it is ironic. But the irony has to do more with the fact that E.U. formed primarily to compete with the USA economically. It is ironic that they are using the language of their chief economic enemy.

However, even this irony must teach China a lesson. If E.U., formed in chief economic competition against the USA, is using English, there is a good reason for this. China can learn from E.U.'s tactical maneuver to compete effectively in the global market. Indeed, E.U.'s practice is better understood in light of the fact that English is the functional commerce language in international business and international law.

China must, therefore, update its English program. It is a common knowledge for all outside of China that China has a horrible English program. Perhaps, there has been changes in recent years to prove this assumption wrong. But by in large, evidence seems scarce that shows China as making great strides in its English education. Changes can be made. And it should be made.

Consider this. It was around 1979 that South Korea officially kicked off its English program in elementary schools. It has taken a while to implement mandatory English programs even with an official policy. And Korea is a mere speck in

China's big face. Consider the kind of work needed to update China's English program. It will take more effort, energy, resources, and time. But this is important. Korea's mandatory English program opened many doors for common Koreans and is seen as directly tied to the Korean boom. An effective English program for China will pay China dividends.

My primary suggestion for China's updating of its English program is to use its Hong Kong residents. Most of the Hong Kong educated speak English fluently. Many of them probably can teach English like a native English speaker. The fact that they know Chinese makes them especially well-suited to be employed for the sake of Chinese educational reform.

The problem is always tied to effective resource management. China has many resources, which are not effectively maximized. Hong Kong is a good example. But we recognize the difficult-ties facing Beijing.

First, there is the question of pay. What kind of pay will entice Hong Kong residents to move to other parts of China to teach English? Whatever that cost may be, China should investi-gate it and plan a strategic resource management based on the research outcome. Using Hong Kong residents is probably the maximal way of using resources. They are all Chinese citizens and speak the language. I should think that although the cost of hiring Hong Kong residents to teach in other parts of China may be high, it will be manageable and certainly a good (if not a necessary) investment.

The cost of hiring Westerners to teach in China would most likely be at least twice as much if not up to ten times as much. Japan's case indicates the potential cost of hiring Westerners to teach English. Perhaps, Japan is incredibly generous to foreigners even if such incentives may not be needed. Still the fact remains that hiring Hong Kong residents will certainly be cost effective even if we take other factors, such as similarity in culture, out of the equation for why China should aggressively push for this type of program to be implemented in its educational reform.

These are, to be sure, cost effective ways to hire Westerners. It may not be a bad idea to examine these possibilities since having choices is a good thing. One less expensive way of hiring Westerners is to give local teacher's pay to missionaries. If there is an open door policy, then there will be many Western missionaries. Many of them will be native English speakers. Even those who may not be native English speakers (such as German missionaries) would probably be fluent enough in English to teach English at an elementary, junior and senior high school levels. This option is particularly attractive because missionaries would already be there and getting them to teach one hour or two per day at a local school would probably be pretty easy. In terms of maximizing the cost-benefit, this may be ideal because China can just pay a respectable hourly wage.

Although using missionaries already in China is probably the most inexpensive way of implementing western teachers in Chinese schools, there are other options as well. One program can involve one year or one term program that uses rotating teachers. Many westerners like to take a few months off and travel. This trend is particularly popular among Australians and New Zealanders. If there is a program in place to provide housing, food, and modest pay for 6 months, you may attract these westerners who want to travel to Asia.

This program will necessitate a rigid structure for teaching. For instance, there should be set textbooks that the teachers use and strict guidelines as to what materials should be covered and why. This is important since you are expecting teachers to change every 6 months.

Furthermore, such a program will need to be mostly conversation focused rather than grammar or literature based. A recommended model program is the "French in Action" program that many American institutions use to teach French. This emersion program uses the philosophy that language instruction should be conversation focused. From day one, only French is basically used. Students watch a video installment and the teacher engages students in French conversation afterwards.

Such a type of program can be designed by Chinese academics. Having a TV with video teaching sessions is not too difficult. And such sessions can be followed by conversation programs with Western teachers. Also, if the course is designed to be more current-situation based, English speakers will not need knowledge of English literature to teach. For instance, the program can be designed for the teachers to talk to students about the West or their own country and history. Allowing a certain flexibility within the structured program for teachers to maximize their background will reduce stress for teachers and students and maximize the learning experience.

Another way to incorporate Western teachers into the Chinese education system is to develop a type of incentive program with Western corporations. Since China is in the beginning of the process of formulating a comprehensive policy on foreign investment and actually holds the cards regarding who gets in and profits from China, China is in a good position to stipulate the conditions. As a policy, China can tie its English program to corporate incentives. It has generally not been done in other Asian countries, but that does not mean China can't do it. In fact, China can lead in terms of holding corporations up to a type of social responsibility.

A possible stipulation can be that each company that sets up a plant must provide X number of hours of English instruction at area high schools, for instance. This condition can be met (1) either by a company's own Western workers providing teaching; (2) a company hiring and bringing in English teachers; (3) a company locating possible teachers in the area who are Westerners (such as wives or husbands of business personel) whom they can pay to teach. So the companies will put up the money and each school will guide the instruction. The company pay can be set up to go through municipal or federal channels, or through the school itself. A policy statement and related laws should, of course, be clearly outlined and disclosed publicly and prominently.

There is another solution besides using Hong Kong residents and temporary western visitors. China can hire other Asians who are English speaking. Obvious country choices are India, Pakistan, Malaysia, the Philippines, and Singapore, all of which basically have English as an understood second primary language.

There are problems with this solution, however, and they should be discussed first. As China's English program will be extensive, it will require thousands of teachers. Having thousands, even tens of thousands, flooding into China who may potentially want to stay permanently may not be what China wants.

China, with its growing economy, must expect English teachers from Asian countries to seriously consider moving permanently to China and wanting a Chinese citizenship. If China is prepared to do this (or even offer the citizenship as an incentive), then inviting Asian teachers who speak English is a good solution.

To put the situation in perspective, it should be noted that China may potentially have to issue citizenships to a hundred thousand or more new immigrants immediately. Many teachers will come with their families. If China follows this route, China should efficiently modify its laws and also set up infrastructure to handle this.

Issuing temporary visas to Asian teachers may be a possible solution, but we are faced with growing ramifications of migrant workers.

Countries that have had a long history of migrant workers generally had them settling down with their working visas and turned a blind eye. China should recognize, therefore, that even without issuing citizenships, China will most likely face a type of *de facto* immigration. China will have to deal with Asian teachers who marry local citizens. And foreign Asian teachers will send their kids to local schools, and they may eventually want to stay in China. Thinking that issuing temporary visas to hundreds of thousands of educated individuals and assuming that they will return after years of teaching without protest could be problematic.

China will also have to contend with potential problems rising with neighboring countries. A couple of years ago, Hong Kong faced a public/international relations fiasco over Filipino house-help. Many of Hong Kong's wealthy used Filipino labor because it was inexpensive compared to using local help. Hong Kong wanted to decrease the number of Filipinos in the city and passed a policy to encourage hiring local help.

What Hong Kong did not understand was that once you let them in, you can't just discard them like yesterday's trash. Filipino workers protested in thousands resulting in the Filipino president issuing statements and the Filipino government looking to retaliate against Hong Kong in a type of tit-for-tat. Hong Kong and the Philippines have long been friends and have benefited from the friendship. However, one situation over migrant workers threatened to make friends into enemies.

Hong Kong was naïve to think that Filipino workers would just leave and go back to the Philippines. Filipino workers have been working for many years in Hong Kong, and they had no jobs to go back to in the Philippines. One or two Filipinos is one thing, but thousands is another.

Also, many Filipino families in the Philippines became dependent on the salary of the Filipinos in Hong Kong. Although Hong Kong residents paid less for Filipino help than for local Chinese help, still the pay was far greater than what an average Filipino earned back home. It is a common practice for Filipinos to send pay back home, and it is a common social phenomena that many Filipinos become dependent on this help. If a few thousand Filipinos are sent back, it not only affects the few thousand, but probably it would affect over one hundred thousand Filipinos in the Philippines either directly or indirectly.

China has to learn from this experience. If they choose to go the route of hiring Asians, they should probably expect them to stay for good. They can't expect them to go back to their countries. Given the Chinese economic progress, most Asians, with the possible exception of Singapore, will find it financially attractive (and in other ways) to stay permanently in China.

I don't discourage using Asian help. In fact, I highly recommend it. If China is wise, this can be a good tool to foster positive relationships with its neighbors. However, China must be aware of the potential threat if it mismanages its foreign labor force, and China must recognize the potential for deep changes in its internal social structure. With adequate preparation, using Asian teachers can perhaps be the best option.

I should say a word or two more about the curriculum. English curriculum should be implemented from elementary to high school levels with a focus on the Chinese masses. While learning English literature is important, it can be learned in translation. The purpose of the English program at the level of up to high school should focus primarily on communication. The English program should be geared toward raising the ability of the citizens to understand English and communicate in English. Reading ability is also important but it does not have to be particularly advanced. Even in America, the reading level for the general population is quite low. My proposal for the implementation of an effective English program for China has functionalist and practical goals.

Simply put, China should implement English programs for its core school curriculum so that it could allow Chinese people to compete on a global level and survive in international contexts more effectively. Anyone seeking a deeper study or more academic study can seek out such venues. For now, China must focus on functionalist and practical goals. Once these are met, China can expand its scope.

Having discussed how and why China should have a better English program, I now turn my attention to other areas of educational reform. I would also advise China to implement greater teaching of Western classics in China's elementary to high school curriculum. While I see the value of having Greek and Latin in China's best schools, my recommendation is again more practical and functionalist. The ultimate goal of introducing Western classics in the Chinese curriculum is to make Chinese masses more informed about the West so they can compete more effectively in international contexts. Thus, language instruction in Greek and Latin may be helpful, but more relevant is the teaching of classical history and literature using the local language. That way China will better understand what makes the world tick. As Americans like to say, "Know your enemy."

During the height of the cold war, the American government poured millions of dollars into studying the Russian language, culture, civilization, etc. Americans firmly believed that if you don't know your enemy (or your competition), you will lose. As one famous western philosopher said, "Knowledge is power." Russia is basically western and shares the basic foundation with the USA. So while America recommended a specialized inquiry into Russia, most Americans understood Russians as westerners with western premises. No special education had to be set apart for America's elementary to senior high in order to gain a better understanding of "the enemy." Also, Russia was not competing in the global market, so individual American citizens did not need knowledge of Russia to compete effectively in the global market back then.

The situation in China is vastly different. Not only is China thrown into the Western arena, which is foreign to the Chinese experience and history, any Chinese individual engaged in any kind of serious economic competition will have to wade through competition in the West. Most likely, they will have to place themselves within the Western arena to compete globally.

Given this reality, it is crucial that China implements into its core curriculum a way of understanding the West. Whereas Western culture is implicitly known for those who grow up in the West, Western culture is foreign to a typical Chinese. While studying individual Western country or culture could be helpful, it may be more practical and effective to teach the foundation of Western culture whose imprint is felt in every Western country, whether Russia or the USA.

By this, I refer to the classics. The classical world (and by this, I mean Greco-Roman) holds the key to western civilization. Ideas found in Greco-Roman philosophy is the core of all western philosophical inquiry. Western institutions are fundamentally based on Greco-Roman institutions. If you understand the classics, you understand the framework of every western nation and culture. Basically, learning the classics can be seen as learning to fish. As the American saying goes, "If you give a man a fish, he will eat for a day, but if you teach a man how to fish, he will eat for life."

In our case, teaching French history is akin to giving a fish. You will have to give fish every time and spoon-feed. But if you teach classics, you give your students the key to understanding every western culture.

How should western classics be taught? I would recommend teaching history and literature. History can be divided into the Roman Republic and the Roman Empire. These two periods can easily occupy one year of intense teaching as there are in them origins of many institutions and institutional changes that are essential to understanding the Western political process that require careful examination. I would encourage particularly focusing on the idea of the relationship between the Senators and the supreme leader. This permutation goes through changes and it is in the very changes that history is made in the ancient world. This reality is not so different today, let's say in the USA or in the UK. Basic principles certainly still hold as well as the institutional mechanics.

Another area of recommended focus is the use of propaganda by the emperors in the Empire, with a particular attention to Augustus. This topic has been a source of thousands of Ph.D.'s and for a good reason. It was the most effective propaganda campaign in Western history. Every successful Western leader, both good and evil, has modeled himself (or herself) after Augustus. Those who understood him and were able to copy him in their context were always successful in exerting great influence. As it is a given fact that many western leaders intentionally model themselves after Augustus, it would not be a mistake to say that understanding his reign opens the door to understanding Western political aspiration and rule.

In terms of literature, I would encourage China to focus on epics and love stories/poems. Chinese scholars may find this recommendation strange. But I would argue that the Chinese focus on military texts actually creates a great weakness in their understanding of the West and Western politics.

Consider the story of Helen of Troy or Penelope. These are stories of love that have political consequences. Whether they were factual or not, these stories are important in showing popular values and motivations. Whereas Asians are hard pressed to find a story of nations fighting over love, as it is not an Asian virtue, westerners elevate love over other virtues, more often than not. This is particularly pointed out in the Roman saying, "Love conquers all." No Asian would say this if he is grounded in the Asian culture. Asians would, without doubt, sacrifice love for duty. This is the Confucian way.

So, when I say epic, I am not saying epic in the same way Asians understand epic, focusing on military aspects. Chinese teachers have to focus on the love aspect of the epic not merely for its romance value or art form but in order to understand fundamental Western motivations and conflicting values.

In my support, I will point out the historical account of Caesar. Caresar was a popular emperor who loved a non-Roman. Love of someone outside of his religion and piety was unacceptable in the context of ancient Rome. Not only did Romans look to their emperors for political and military victories, they looked to the emperor to maintain the Roman religion. Ronald Mellor's Ph.D. thesis on the goddess Roma highlights the input of the Imperial Cult. For Caesar to love Cleopatra, who neither observed Roman piety nor paid allegiance to Rome, was treachery. And Caesar's enemies made sure that they highlighted this interpretation.

Caesar was truly a man in love. For, Caesar was not stupid and understood his society and the ramifications of his actions. Caesar understood Cleopatra's intentions to share his rule and have their love child obtain the rightful crown of the Roman Empire. Like a man in love, Caesar allowed Cleopatra's ostentatious show of affection and her presence in Rome, which certainly agitated the Senatorial ruling class. By bringing Cleopatra to Rome, Caesar knew the insult he was heaping on Rome as words of Senatorial discontent certainly must have reached his ears through his friends and advisers. But Caesar was willing to sacrifice for his love.

In an ironic sense, Caesar was truly being a Roman since Romans emphasized and elevated friendship and love. Romans believed in the concept of commitment and obligations to their friends and lovers. It is not surprising that when Roman soldiers occupying Roman provinces married local women, they became Romans by marriage with full rights of a Roman citizenship. By in large, Americans have adopted this principle without question. Not all countries easily extend citizenship on account of marriage.

But ironically it was because, as one devoted to Roman virtues, he refused to dishonor Cleopatra that Caesar wrote his own death sentence. Senators probably could not have organized to kill Caesar without his commitment to Cleopatra. The Senators probably could not have convinced Caesar's best friend Brutus to join in the conspiracy unless they could impress upon Brutus that Caesar's ties to Cleopatra jeopardized Rome and the Roman people whom they were supposed to represent.

Love as a value was so prominent in ancient Rome that Cleopatra spelled demise of not one top ruler but two. Even as he saw his friend's political career and life come to an abrupt end on account of his love for Cleopatra, Mark Anthony duly followed in Caesar's footsteps. For outside readers, this smacks of pure idiocy. Why would anyone love a woman who (1) undoes a political leader, (2) clearly symbolizes something that is distasteful to the Roman Senatorial class, and (3) raises collective passions and unifies enemies to bring about a powerful leader's demise?

Mark Anthony was not an idiot. He was well-educated in history and literature, well-versed on the rules of the Roman society, and well-aware of why the Senators were able to kill Caesar in the Senate. The situation may be akin to George Bush's. If President Bush aggressively supports Israel when many Americans blame Israel's peace-adverse policies against Palestinians as a reason that propelled the September 11th attack and thrust America into an unwanted war with a couple of Middle Eastern countries, the Senators who oppose

Bush can more easily bring about the end of George Bush and his loyalists. But George Bush did not remain faithful to his Cleopatra, as his attacks on Israel's policies and taking away of public funds and UN vote-support for Israel show. Bush lives and thrives because he stabbed Israel on the back.

But George Bush is a political pragmatist, and this is a virtue in a democratic USA. In Rome it was different. You did not discard your friends because they were a political liability. That would have gone against the highest of Roman *virtus* and *pietas*. Caesar was true to the Roman value system and did not betray it despite being infatuated with an Egyptian woman. Neither did Mark Anthony act with treachery toward his love.

Mark Anthony fulfilled his obligation as a friend and lover to Cleopatra, fully aware of the implications and knowing that it was probable that he would meet the same end as Julius Caesar. And many have idealized and glorified this prominent Roman's love for an Egyptian leader, who neither shared Roman religious piety or social values. And the tragedy of two lovers from two different worlds committing suicide together with poison might have been an inspiration for Shakespeare's tale of Romeo and Juliet who came from different worlds and died together by the same means. Just as Shakespeare and the world found powerful romance in tragic love, many in the ancient world probably saw a romantic value in Mark Anthony's love for one who was not a Roman.

But the fact remains. A Roman in the noble class cannot love one who does not share Roman *pietas* without consequences. As a prominent figure and a type of symbol for Romans and the Roman religion, Mark Anthony wrote his own death years before it happened. If Romans killed the *princeps* who loved a woman who did not share Roman piety, then you can expect the Romans to kill a Senator who loves a woman who does not share Roman piety. For Romans, the destiny of the Roman Empire depended on Roman religious piety. Even if they themselves remained impious to the Roman religion, they were superstitious enough to believe that their leaders must be pious to Roman gods, and not Egyptians'. Even if they were lazy and did not often sacrifice to Roman gods, Romans feared the possible retaliation of Roman gods due to their leader's impiety.

This Roman superstition can be better understood in the context of worshipping the *genus* of the *Imperator*. The household god of the Roman royal family was revered and respected by ordinary Romans who may have had their own household gods. Even as they worshipped their household patron gods, they made a point of recognizing the importance of the Imperial *genus* for the good of Rome and their personal safety. Romans understood that the Roman Imperial household that did not honor the *genus* and elevate Roman piety would bring about the destruction of Rome and that they too may be killed in the anger of the gods.

The fact that Caesar and Mark Anthony ignored the superstitions of ordinary Romans for their love may win some brownie points with teenage women in love with love. And it probably won the joy of Egyptians in Egypt and the Egyptians in the Diaspora. But how many Egyptians were there in Rome, far away from the Egyptian State? The fact that Caesar and Mark Anthony won the favor of the Egyptians in Rome is glossed over or ignored by Roman historians. Roman historians describe a fascination that Romans had with Cleopatra and her elephants entering Rome. However, there is acerbic satire and sarcasm coloring the pages of ancient Roman historians as any elementary student of Latin can tell you.

It is possible that Caesar and Mark Anthony had *hubris*, a type of trust in self-prominence and the security of their place in the Roman upper class. Perhaps, pro-Egyptian factions buzzed and encouraged such a mistaken perception of their security. Modern historians writing about the past have not dismissed the idea that these leaders might have been drunk on power. Some historians describe how Caesar took on god-like attributes and even acted like an Oriental King. They argue that it was the Roman hatred of kings that attracted their hatred of Caesar, looking more and more like a king.

Although there may be some indication even from classical sources of such an interpretation, the fact is that Caesar did not aggressively seek to be a king in Rome. This is an important fact. Caesar knew he could rule as a *dictator* with kingly powers as long as he did not try to destroy Roman institutions. Even Augustus, who was a successful ruler who lived a long life, encouraged his attribution of king and even deification in the provinces (but not in Rome). This did not disturb the Romans one bit. As long as Augustus did not proclaim himself as a king in Rome or destroy Roman institutions, Romans could tolerate what he did outside of Rome. Romans were concerned with the protection of their institutions and the way things were in Rome. Romans cared about Roman gods and the piety to the Roman gods. If Caesar and Mark Anthony even put up a front that expressed aggressive piety towards Roman gods and Roman institutions, they would not have met their end. Moreover, they should not have accentu-ated the fact that they took one who was not loyal to the Roman gods as their wife. They gave this impression and disturbed many Romans. Romans cared about their institutions.

It is like modern-day Britain. Many people may not necessarily like the nobility, but when Labour leaders try to destroy the Hereditary Peerage system and confront the Monarchy, the British people become discontent and the society experiences instability. Now, even Labour mem-bers are beginning to be deeply discontent about the efforts of some Labour leaders attacking Britain's historic institutions and come to the defense of the Monarchy as one that the people choose to uphold. The Monarchy system is an important and a stabilizing symbol in Britain and the British people are superstitious about it. That is why they turned out in millions at the funeral of Princess Diana and the Queen Mother. They may say this or that off the cuff about the Monarchy, but when it comes down to the deep sentiment of the British people, they know that they will all lose something of themselves in the destruction of the Monarchy. They are superstitious enough to fear what might happen to them if the Monarchy is destroyed. This is the same kind of superstitious fear that the Romans had about their institutions. The consequences for Blair and his fellow leaders are yet to be seen, but as peaceful as the British people are, if Blair is again chosen to power, it would not be surprising to see a rare assassination attempt on his life and the lives of his children and wife. For people act out of their "superstition" and the fear for their personal safety when core institutions are attacked, especially by national leaders.

Just as Romans sacrificed their beloved leaders, the British are capable of sacrificing Blair and his family to preserve their superstitious sense of British safety and future. The history of humankind has shown again and again not to mess with local institutions where superstitious devotions play any role.

Caesar's and Mark Anthony's love story is therefore more compelling. They knew most likely in concrete terms what their love of one impious to the Roman gods meant. But they embraced death. They privileged the Roman value of friendship and love over the Roman value of piety to the gods. But even within the Roman system, it is clear that piety to the gods was far more important than friendship or love. They privileged a lesser value and paid for it.

Augustus, Julius Caesar's son, did not make the mistake his father made. Augustus was careful to elevate the Roman gods and encourage Roman piety. In fact, Augustus legislated piety and put beyond the shadow of doubt that he was loyal to the Roman religion. No one could have doubted that Augustus honored Roman gods as he aggressively displayed his piety. Augustus' aggressive show of piety won the hearts of the Roman people and their loyalty. Even non-practicing Romans expected their leaders to be pious to the Roman gods. It is like an Irish Catholic who lives in London.

The Irish Catholic might have not gone to mass in 3 years. The Irish Catholic might not have gone to Confessions in 5 years. He might not have done anything resembling his Catholic identity for 2 years. He may live a life of a sinner by Catholic standards. He may even attack and criticize the church on occasions. But this Irish Catholic will expect the local bishop to honor Christian theology and practice. Even if he supports homosexual marriage personally, he would not consider it right that the Bishop supports homosexual marriage. His assumption is based on his superstitious fear of God's retribution when religious leaders violate God's law for social order.

You would be hard-pressed to find a non-practicing Catholic who thinks that God approves homosexual marriage in the Bible. It's one thing for a non-practicing Catholic to say and do, it is wholly another thing for a Catholic Bishop to oppose the stated position in the Bible when everyone can read it in print. This explains the superstitious element of Irish Catholics in London. And in fact it is not just with Irish Catholics. Most people have a different standard for what position the church should officially hold and what people personally do. To err is human, as the saying goes.

It was this way in Rome. Not all Romans were pious but they expected their official leaders to be. Not all Romans readily defended Roman gods against insults, but they expected Roman leaders to fight to the death to defend the honor of the Roman gods. Romans retracted their support from Caesar and Mark Anthony when they perceived that they were favoring Egyptian gods and trying to portray Roman gods as almost equal to or inferior to Egyptian gods. Even though the Romans disliked Caesar's and Mark Anthony's enemies, they preferred that their current leaders die rather than see their Roman gods slandered and downgraded from the supreme position.

Roman actions mirrored popular sentiment, generally. Any respected leader could easily be dragged down if he is perceived to be not defending people's gods. It doesn't matter how much titles he has, how powerful he was before, what kind of connections or important friends he has. Romans wanted their gods honored and defended. They cared less about transgressions and sexual practices of their leaders, as long as they fought to keep their gods' place at top. That's how most people think. Gods are gods and humans are humans.

A good illustration of this sentiment of people is illustrated in Rev. Jimmy Swaggart. He preaches enthronement of God and of Heaven and eternal damnation. He was arguably the most powerful tele-evangelist of the 1980s. People were even personally loyal to him because they believed he honored Jesus and defended the kingdom of Christ.

Some of his enemies hired private investigators and dug up dirt on him. Rev. Swaggart was exposed of having sex regularly with a member of his staff who was not his wife. Most of Rev. Swaggart's enemies thought that he would be destroyed because of his sexual sins. Pious clergy attacked what they called "impious actions."

What his political enemies miscalculated was that it actually strengthened Rev. Swaggart's position to remind people of Rev. Swaggart's sin. Ordinary people felt that they could identify with Rev. Swaggart. Almost 50 per cent of all Americans have committed adultery in the form of premarital sex or extramarital sex. It's important for them to know that Christ forgives adultery when you repent. It's their personal salvation at stake. The more pastors who never supposedly committed adultery attacked Rev. Swaggart personally for sexual transgressions, the more American people came to his defense. These pastors were damning every American who ever had premarital or extramarital sex. It's one thing to talk about sexual purity as a biblical principle, it is completely another thing to take potshots, either directly or indirectly, at a Christian leader who had committed a sin, but was now willing to submit to God's law.

Rev. Swaggart repented for his many sexual transgressions and asked Christ's mercy and continued on preaching. Many actually were converted to Christianity as a result. Many prostitutes and others living in lives of sin assume that their sins are too great for Christ to forgive because they see that no one around them is forgiving them. Rev. Swaggart's case showed them, the "untouchables," that Christ can accept prostitutes and sinners and forgive them and others who commit great sins. If Christ can forgive a Christian leader who committed multiple sexual sins, He could certainly forgive me, a little nobody, who has sinned. Rev. Swaggart and other tele-evangelists and their sins/repentance propelled a wave of popular conversions.

Obviously, Rev. Swaggart was able to maintain and enlarge his authority because he recognized and preached that adultery is sinful. It further helped his Christian authority that he preached aggressively against homosexuality. Especially in light of "blameless" clergy condoning homosexuality in church either via silence or explicitly, Rev. Swaggart enjoyed popular power over and against established churches and their leaders. Churches in the US that really enjoy such popular power are equally aggressively anti-homosexual in preaching and explicit teaching, such as the Southern Baptists and the Roman Catholics.

It has always been the case that whatever one's actions, as long as piety's ultimate right is asserted and the honor of the local gods privileged and defended to the point of death, the leader will maintain popular loyalty to his person. This fact has never failed any point in the history in the West.

Augustus understood this principle and legislated morality to privilege the Roman religion. In his personal practice, he showed himself loyal to the gods. He pictured himself loyal to the gods through propaganda. He pictured himself as one who would fight to defend the honor of the Roman gods. Unlike his father, Augustus was not going to allow the Roman gods to bow down and submit to the gods of another people as if divine authority of the Roman gods were annulled by subservience. Augustus' privileging the dominance of the Roman gods won him solid support and the loyalty of the masses, even those who did not actually practice piety.

Augustus clearly shows the role that piety played in his rule. *Res Gestae* is filled with his efforts to honor the gods, to prop up traditional institutions, and to renovate those elements in Roman society tied to Roman popular superstition. Augustus understood the relationship between popular religiosity and political rule.

One can argue that the reason why George Bush is so popular is that he is perceived as pious in the same way that Augustus was. It is no secret that George Bush was a party animal at Yale University and frequently has been seen drunk in the past. It is no secret that Bush junior, born into privilege, did a lot of frivolous things that many children of privilege do. Even now, everyone knows Bush is privileged and always will be.

Whereas some may expect the working class and the immigrants to hate him for his privilege, the opposite has happened. Rarely has a Republican

President enjoyed the support of the people of color and immigrants that George Bush enjoys. Rarely has a president enjoyed the support of the working class, many of whom hate the privileged classes to which Bush belongs.

The explanation is simple. Like a genius in tune with ancient history, Bush did exactly what Augustus did. Bush emphasized piety to the American God – Christ. Bush is very public about honoring Christ. The more he does this, the more even non-practicing Christians seem to be won over. Whereas if Bush did not aggressively honor Christ, it would be difficult to find loyalty in the working class, the fact that Bush honors their God makes the working class loyal to Bush in phenomenal ways.

The working class is far more superstitious than the upper class. They belive that Christ holds the key not only to America's future but also to their personal safety. The fact that George Bush honors Christ, as Augustus did the traditional Roman gods, makes all of his other weaknesses seem irrelevant to many in the American working class who perceive that Christ is becoming more and more displeased with the anti-Christian direction of the American government. In essence, his pro-Christ stance makes Bush to be the people's representative, almost outside of the corrupt American political and legal systems that have legislated against the church and church members.

For instance, pro-abortion laws are seen by American Catholics as an attack on Christ. The Pope issued a papal decree forbidding Catholic priests from giving communion to political leaders who support abortion. The Pope is acting in his capacity to defend the law of Christ. This is a resounding support of Bush and his aggressive anti-abortion stance, as John Kerry, an Irish Catholic, supports pro-abortion laws. No Catholic priest in America or elsewhere can give communion to John Kerry. It is a type of an excommunication or a step from excommunication. To the Vatican, John Kerry is not a Catholic. The Vatican is essentially proclaiming its support for Bush and encouraging that Irish Catholics vote for Bush and not Kerry. The Vatican supports Bush because he supports the Vatican policy on abortion. Kerry defies the Vatican and Church Law, and for that the Vatican considers Kerry to be excommunication-worthy.

In essence, it is safe to assume that John Kerry will be going to Hell by Catholic law, unless he changes his position on abortion. No priest is allowed to offer John Kerry communion. And a priest who does offer John Kerry communion can be excommunicated and sent to Hell. Kerry will not be eligible for proper last rites. Kerry cannot in all honesty call himself a Catholic if the Vatican bars him directly from communion. He is a pagan, and no Christian who respects the Vatican owes him allegiance.

The power of respecting the Christian God in the West is an intangible (often not discussed) issue with real consequences. A US Senator from Pennsylvania publicly condemned homosexuality as unnatural and equal to having sex with an animal. Even Democratic Senators refused to attack this Catholic Senator aggressively. Bush showed him his full support and began to push to outlaw homosexual marriage as a constitutional amendment. American people came to the Catholic Senator's defense and more and more Baptists are voting for practicing Catholics as the result of such an anti-homosexual position of this prominent Catholic Senator.

In fact, it would not be wrong to say that practicing Catholics in the USA have won the hearts of the American Protestant majority through their anti-abortion and anti-homosexuality positions. In fact, Baptists and Catholics are now strong political allies trying to outlaw homosexual marriage and abortion. Baptists have killed to stop abortion and it's not inconceivable that a civil war might break out if America does not overturn some of its anti-Christian policies.

The success of popular working class movements, such as *Promise Keepers* and the Fundamentalist books of the *Left Behind* series, show that working class, popular Christian devotion is at an all time high and is reaching an explosion point.

Bush understands the popular sentiment of the American working class and has been effective copying Augustus in portraying himself as devoted to the American God.

Popular piety in England shows that the situation in England is not so different from America. England attests that many of its immigrants revere Jesus. The African community is mostly Christian and many of them are aggressively evangelical. The Caribbean community is almost all Christian, many of them very conservative, Charismatic Christians. Many Asians are Christians. Both Hindu and Muslims respect Jesus as a god or a prophet. Only Jews who are not Christians have a lack of respect for "the bastard child." If an English leader showed his piety to Christianity more aggressively and openly, he would win the loyalty of not only England's working class but also immigrants. But Blair is no Bush. Whereas Bush has enjoyed popular support of up to 90 per cent, Blair is fortunate even when 40 per cent of the British public shows him support. Blair fundamentally does not understand Augustus' religio-political program in the days of ancient Rome.

Classics holds a key to understanding the West. It is important to understand western values of love and of piety to their God. China, therefore, should teach Western classics, particularly focusing on epics and key leaders in ancient Greece and Rome. As western leaders model themselves after classical rulers, understanding the primary model is essential for any deep understanding of the West, the way Western society functions, and the relationship between rulers and their people. All literature (poems and such) studied should be studied with an attention to this detail.

Besides emphasizing implementing a better English curriculum and introducing a greater study of Western classics, I would also recommend studying Christianity in Chinese schools in a history-type program. To say that Christianity is the single most influential factor in western history is an understatement. Christianity is the beginning of Western civilization as we know it. Yes, ancient Rome and Greece are foundations, but they are forever seen through Christian contexts since the advent of Jesus Christ. Christianity is not only influential, it is the cause of western civilization, institutions, and the arts as we know it.

The impact of Christianity is found in every institution, discipline, trade, and practice in the West. Both popular and intellectual advancement and understanding cannot exist outside of Christianity in the west. This holds true for every western country.

The reality is similar to Confucianism in China and Korea. Confucianism can be described as both a religion and philosophy. But it was not something merely to be studied. Confucianism was taught in Chinese and Korean educational programs for centuries, but it is more important to emphasize that the society was also ordered using the Confucian blueprint.

The Chinese family and the Korean family were ordered through Confucianism. Filial duty and the emphasis on family ties were outlined in Confucian terms of obligations. It was duty more than love that bound a son to his father. Although love was not denigrated, it was not mentioned as a prerequisite for filial duty. Thus, in essence, duty was understood as love, or love was assumed and subsumed under duty.

Filial duty was seen as his most pious obligation in terms of the family. Thus, filial duty was outlined more specifically with advancing time. And it came to be understood socially that it was expected of every son. In fact, a son who did not fulfill his filial duty was seen as bad. The goodness or badness of a man was determined by his fulfillment of obligations as a son. Even if he transgressed in other areas, if he fulfilled his obligations as a son, most likely he would be seen in positive terms. There was not an absolutized concept of good and evil in objective terms in Confucianism, unlike in Christianity. In Christianity, the concept of sin is an objective concept that stands alone regardless of human relationships. A person is sinful because he commits a sin. In Confucianism there are no such objective standards. Morality and sin are seen in terms of people's obligations to each other. Thus, for instance, if a friend kills someone, it would be more "sinful" not to help him escape. Confucianism obligates a friend to help. In fact, a friend who does not help his murderer friend escape is disrespected in a Confucian society and is seen as a "sinner." It is clear that the Confucian world-view is quite different.

For the purpose of this essay, it does not help to try to determine which system is more "good" or "righteous." It is a fact that the Confucian system undergirds Asian societies. This is an objective, factual statement. Confucianism is an important part of the Asian culture. It is, therefore, important to understand it. Even if one wants to change the Asian culture, it is impossible to do so in the long-run without the willingness to understand Confucianism in its own terms.

It is the same way with Christianity. Christianity should be understood in its own terms. The Western society has fundamentally been shaped by Christianity. To put a value judgment of whether it is good or bad that Western society is shaped by Christianity is a futile exercise if one is engaged in endeavors to understand the West.

If China and the Chinese people fail to understand Christianity, China will certainly fail to understand the West and Westerners. Even Western economic system of Capitalism was an outgrowth of Christian principles and has the Christian theology as its foundation. Without the Christian experience and history, it would have been impossible to usher in Capitalism in the West. Max Weber's attestation of Calvinistic influences on Capitalism must be taken with all seriousness.

Calvinism was a movement named after John Calvin, a French Reformer. Although he is viewed by many as a Protestant Christian leader and thinker *par excellence*, John Calvin saw himself as a part of Christian history and in the tradition of the Roman Catholic Church. John Calvin never denied that Christ worked through the Roman Catholic Church. It shows that even Reformation leaders like John Calvin and Martin Luther saw a fundamental continuation of Christian history and experience in the West.

The impact of Christianity in the West cannot be minimized. Besides economic institutions, Christianity undergirds political institutions. It should not be surprising given that Christianity was the official religion of the Holy Roman Empire since the days of Theodotius in the 4th century AD. The emperor decreed by law that Christianity should be embraced actively by the Western country.

In a sense, embracing of religion was not a Christian invention. The Romans embraced pagan religion as their official religion before the birth of Jesus Christ in Bethlehem. While the pan-religious structure may already have been in place, it was Christianity and Christian leaders who were able to thoroughly Christianize the empire. The Catholic Church was able effectively to make an active infrastructure for the Christian Church even in the smallest villages.

Marc Bloch writes effectively about the local parish and its structures during the high Middle Ages. Where official church units failed to reach, itinerant Christians were effective. The best example of this was the Mendicant movement of the 12th Century. Franciscans and Dominicans multiplied and were seen in the countryside. These Christian monks took vows of poverty and went from town to town preaching Jesus Christ and salvation through him. As they renounced wealth and possession, they had to beg for food and lodging. A term "holy begging" is somewhat used to describe what the Franciscans and the Dominicans did.

Some have done comparative studies of the Mendicant orders and the Cynics of the Greco-Roman world over 1,000 years ago. There does seem to be similarities in the way Cynics, such as the founder Diogenes, went about "preaching" in public and going from town to town begging to sustain himself.

Although there are similarities, it may be a bit far-fetched to draw a causative link due to lapse in time. More likely is the possibility that the Mendicant orders represented a development in the long tradition of monastic movements. Benedictine monks few centuries before likewise started to take a vow of poverty. Although they were in monasteries, there was an emphasis on labor and activity. Monks also emphasized helping the poor and meeting the needs of the Christian laity.

St. Francis developed these values to justify a more aggressive intrusion into society to meet the needs of the laity. Coming from the educated, wealthy elite, St. Francis had the proper education to compel him to think seriously about history and society. He was in the right circles to know what the elites in Medieval Europe were failing to do to meet the needs of ordinary people. Unlike his other wealthy, elite friends and family, St. Francis actively took steps to rectify the situation. What began as a small local movement spread throughout the Christian Empire. Although local clergy threatened to destroy the Franciscans and even brought charges against them to excommunicate them, the Fourth Lateran Council in 1215 exonerated their value in the Church. With official approval and the encouragement of the Vatican, the Mendicant orders were able to rejuvenate the Christian Church. Some historians have argued that the Mendicant orders saved Christendom. They were particularly effective in reinvigorating Christian piety and loyalty among the poor and the working class.

Many social programs in the West have been deeply influenced by monastic movements and their impact on church institutions is clearly visible. One can argue that secular social programs in the West actually evidence a smooth transition from what the Christian Church was doing. As Europe's governments came to have more independence from the church and started to limit the church, the church no longer had the means to help the poor as directly as in the Middle Ages. Governments took over Christian models. The fact that government officials were Christian certainly was instrumental in the imputing of Christian elements in Western social programs.

Western institutions were certainly very much impacted by Christianity. In essence, such key impacts of revival movements, such as monastic movements, allowed Christianity to have a sustained influence.

Another reason was that there was a steady flow of Christian thinkers who engaged society and institutions, including the political, in their writings. In fact, it may not be wrong to state that writing about politics took the most amount of mental space and ink after writing directly about Christian issues. Every major Christian thinker has written something about the Christian view of politics. St. Augustine's *City of God* stands as a monument to Christian political discussion, but he was certainly not alone. Thomas Aquinas wrote actively about politics as well as Erasmus, John Calvin, and Martin Luther.

In England and Scotland, Puritans and Presbyterians actively wrote about Christianity and politics. After the Puritans left England due to persecution by Anglicans, Puritans established themselves eventually in America. From Harvard and Yale, Puritans wrote to create a Christian vision for America.

The majority of Puritan writings emphasize that Christians are the chosen people of God. In fact, Puritans wrote of Christians in America as a type of Joshua's Conquest of Canaan. God had given Christians in America the responsibility of conquering the Land. Using the language of Christian Holy War based on the themes of the Old Testament – particularly the Exodus and the Conquest – America's Christians engaged in active efforts to conquer the Land. Many Puritans did not have a problem with genocide since they were modeling themselves after ancient Israelites who completely annihilated the inhabitants in the Land that they wanted to conquer.

Christians not only described themselves as the true people of God, they perceived America as the City on a Hill in Augustinian terms. The perception that Christians as God's people had the rights to commit genocide and conquer Land is known as "The Manifest Destiny." This sentiment is very much a part of the American psyche.

American Christians do not have a problem with genocide as such. American Christians never apologized for their genocides in wars because they believe (still) that a Holy War justifies genocides on the model of Joshua's War in the Old Testament. It was because Americans have no problem with genocides in wars that they were able to drop Atom Bombs on the innocent people of Japan in World War 2.

Even today, Americans by in large have no problem with genocides in the context of a Holy War. That is the reason why Americans embraced Germans right after World War 2. Most Americans have no real problem with Germans having killed 6 million Jews. It seems like Americans care because there is so much Nazi-bashing in academia. While Americans saw Nazis as political enemies, most Americans hate Jews as "Christ-killers." They do not hate Germans. Nazis were a political enemy during the war like the British during the Revolutionary War. Most Americans don't see the difference between the British and the Nazis in the context of a war. This explains why America so quickly embraced Germany after the war. It was in fact the Germans who were hitting themselves over the head after the war. Americans fundamentally believe, according to the principles of The Manifest Destiny, that genocides are acceptable in the context of a war. What a few intellectuals may write in opposition does not undo hundreds of years of thinking, writing, and policy on the idea of Christians as the people of God who have the right to wage war according to the principles of the Old Testament.

In Europe, Christians have been less aggressive about describing themselves as the people of God. But the Catholic church as well as all Protestant denominations fundamentally believe that Christians are the people of God. The difference is that while the majority believe that God rejected the Jews and damned them as a cursed people after Christ's crucifixion, there are a few Christians who believe that God is trying to get the Jews to repent as the people of God. But by in large only sectarian Christians believe this. The majority of Christians in Europe and America believe that Christians are God's people and if Jews want to be a part of God's people, they have to make a personal commitment to Christ and be baptized. Jews are rejected as a people belonging to God.

In America, this is clearer. In Baptist and Charismatic churches, it is common to hear the pastor end his prayer by saying, "Let all God's people say 'Amen.'" This is an affirmation after every prayer that God rejected the Jews and now Christians are the true people of God. You hear this prayer ending less frequently in Europe, but among "free" churches, it's not uncommon. And the Vatican II affirms the idea that Christians are God's people and Jews are no longer the people of God.

The efforts of the Baptists to convert the Jews in the USA have to be seen in this light. Baptists believe that Jews are rejected by God and will definitely go to the eternal holocaust in Hell. Baptists want to love the enemies of Christ as Christ taught, so they have committed themselves to converting every Jew in America to Christianity. Baptists fundamentally believe Jews should be annihilated for the crime of crucifying Christ. And if Jews were annihilated in America by President Bush's decree, most Baptists will accept it in hindsight as the will of God to punish unrepentant Jews, such as according to the prophecies of Jeremiah.

Baptists want their enemies saved only because Christ commanded Christian love. But if the Jews don't convert to Christianity, you will see little sympathy from a working-class Baptist when Jews are annihilated in America.

The Christian understanding of themselves is often modeled after Old Testament ideas applied to ancient Israelites. Since their identity is bound in text and tradition, it is hard to disassociate them. Especially, it is impossible to change the views of the working-class and normal American Christians who read the Bible to determine their understanding of how God punishes Jews for not repenting and not accepting Christ.

Although elites in Christianity often get more print space, it's hard to deny the overarching power of popular Christian piety and discourse which often do not make it into print (or wide distribution). Further difficult to understand is the implicit assumptions. The example of Jews deserving annihilation for killing Christ is implicitly accepted by most American Christians although never verbalized. It is a fundamental part of how Americans understand themselves and the world.

It is important to study Christianity because it will help China to start understanding implicit assumptions and ingrained values. Certainly, study-ing Christianity actively will allow China to understand the more explicit positions in Christianity and western society. Sometimes, there are difficulties because writing in print does not necessarily reflect popular piety or opinion. Still, studying Christianity as attested in print will give a better understanding of the west and its motivations than not studying it.

China will certainly benefit from focusing on the three areas mentioned above for its educational program reforms. A better English language instruction, an implementation of courses on Western classics, and an effort to understand the Christian experience in the context of China's educational teaching and research will enlighten China's way as China competes in the Western context. China was wise to enter the global market, basically dictated by Western rules, because it can potentially make China the wealthiest nation in the world and allow it to do a lot of good. But not adequately understanding the West or helping Chinese citizens understand the West (and communicate in the Western lingo) can, in fact, jeopardize China in ways that were not possible when China was in economic and political isolation in the past.

CHAPTER 4:

ECONOMICS AND GLOBAL COMPETITION

China has a great obligation particularly in the area of economics. China can make important contributions to global economy and generate growth for all. American economic progress since the Great Depression has shown that a country can rise from absolute poverty of most of its citizens to a state of incredible wealth for most of the populace (in relative terms vis-à-vis the global economy). And American economic progress has fueled growth for Europe and Asia as well. Wealth can be generated, surprisingly enough, from "nowhere."

In the same way, Chinese population can rise to economic wealth in 20-30 years and create a middle class standard that matches American middle class standards, if the Chinese government is smart enough to implement policies that spur growth. Few wise decisions by the government can be the key to economic progress and staying financial power.

I would recommend that China focus on these areas: (1) integrating the Asian market; (2) creating a viable internal financial structure; and (3) encouraging big businesses.

First, I will discuss the issue of integrating the Asian market. It is in China's interest in the long run to see to a viable economic network in Asia. Whether China likes it or not, the Asian market is linked. When the Asian economic crisis hit and Asian markets were completely devastated, one resounding fact presented itself. When one (or more) Asian economy suffers, all economies in Asia are directly affected. Korean and Japanese economies were particularly affected but Indonesian and Philippine markets felt the impact directly. China was not then as affected because it was not really a part of the global economy (within which the Asian economy is a coherent unit), but now if the same devastation were to hit Korea or Japan, the Chinese market would plunge.

It is true that American and other markets were affected as well. But they did not feel the impact to the extent that Asian markets did. It showed that Asian markets were a *de facto* unit in the same way European markets are tied.

The European case may particularly enlighten. European countries realized that European markets are integrally tied. They understood that an adverse turn of a major European market will impact other European markets directly. The realization of the symbolic whole of the European market propelled European countries to devise integratedness of the market in reality, and they sought to legislate the implementation of an integrated market in principle. Thus, the European Union came to receive political powers over individual member countries. An important part of the political structure is the economic oversight of E.U. over member countries. Already there are rigid rules concerning commerce, interest rates, trade, and inflation that member countries are bound to. And E.U. law is gaining more and more power over national laws of member countries.

In fact, framework laws of E.U., in effect, annul member countries' laws and supercede them. More and more cases are rising where E.U. law is used to punish national laws that violate individual rights as seen through the E.U. law framework.

Certainly, the legal dominance of the E.U. federal principle is attested in economic policy. The Euro, the new currency of the European Union, represents the most visible attestation of the policy of integration. The European Union is aggressive about creating a unified structure and this stems from their understanding that they share the same economic fate.

There is a question as to whether such an aggressive integration is a good thing. The United Kingdom and Denmark have so far refused to join the Euro currency although they are a part of the European Union. This may be a wise decision given the current fluctuation of the Euro. The British pound, for instance, has remained relatively stable in the last five years.

In contrast, the Euro has fluctuated significantly. To illustrate this point, the example of the currency exchange rate will suffice. 2 years ago, 100 US dollars was equivalent to about 105 Euros. Now, $100 is equivalent to about 70 Euros. That's about 35% change in the last 2 years. It shows that the Euro is highly unstable as a currency and does not bode well for the long run.

Why is it important for the currency to be relatively stable? It is difficult for foreign countries to engage in commerce with countries whose currency fluctuates so dramatically because real profit margins are harder to predict. It may be possible that companies will have to resort to what they do in 3rd world countries with highly fluctuating currencies. They will have to use US $ rather than the local currency. While third world countries resort to this because they want the business, European countries will be less accepting of such humiliating policies. They will trade in the Euro even if it means it will destroy them. For many European countries, it's about European pride.

In essence, E.U. has put itself in a bind with the Euro. Now that they have destroyed local currencies, they can't really go back to local currencies. More importantly, the Euro policy is an integral part of the E.U. philosophy and system.

In hindsight, Britain and Denmark not joining the Euro probably was wise and beneficial to their own economies. The Euro was probably premature. That is not to say that the Euro can't become stable. But as of now, it is highly unstable and this will cost European countries. In fact, member countries are beginning to see the negative impact of the Euro policy. There is higher inflation that seems uncontrollable. Products cost more now vis-à-vis income, particularly in smaller E.U. states, such as Portugal. It is hurting their economy. Unemployment rates are rising across the board in

Europe because highly unstable Euro means less foreign investment and less job creation. Even German companies are beginning to move their business abroad to more stable environments, and this has to be done partly because of the unstable Euro. The unstable Euro deeply cuts into profit. It is impossible to change the price of a product radically, and the fluctuations in Euro is decreasing German profit, for instance, in the USA by up to 35%.

So, a walkman made by Siemens that cost $100 fetched Siemens 105 Euros 2 years ago. A more advanced model that costs about the same amount of money to produce for Siemens is sold at $100. Had the Euro remained stable, the profit per product would be relatively same. But because of the fluctuation in the Euro, Siemens is making 70 Euros per sale. In fact, the currency fluctuation may result in the German company losing money per product.

Consider this. It costs 10 Euros to make a product. 10 Euros per item is invested in marketing and publicity. 10 Euros in carriage costs and insurance. 10 Euros are used in customer service and communication costs. 10 Euros are paid to the middlemen. 10 Euros are used per product for tax purposes and tariffs. 10 Euros are needed to pay employees and their benefits. 5 Euros are used for research and developments. That's 75 Euros per product. If the product was sold at $100 two years ago, that brought in 35 Euro per product or over 50% profit, which is more than respectable by any standard. 2 years later, the product sold at $100 will bring in 70 Euros, which means that for each product sold, Siemens loses 5 Euros. Siemens cannot change its policies radically or raise product price since it is, in fact, competing with American companies largely based on the US $ standard. This means that Siemens will have to sell at a loss.

It is important for Siemens to maintain its market share and a pool of return customers. To do that, they will have to sell at a loss and go into debt with the hope that the currency situation will turn around. Another solution for Siemens is to bring its factory out of Germany and move it to America. If the company continued to operate in Germany, all would be on the Euro standard for wages, etc. If Germany operated in the USA, they can pay in dollars. If they pay in dollars, production, and marketing costs will be in dollars (equivalent to the $ cost 2 years ago). The profit will be $25. That may only be about 17 Euros (compared to 30 Euros in equivalent profit a couple of years ago), but it is certainly better than selling at a loss of 5 Euros.

And that's exactly what's happening. More and more German companies are moved out of Germany and even out of Europe.

German companies feel compelled to do so because of the unstable Euro. But given the new-ness of the integrated market and the instability of the Euro, this action of German companies will further destabilize the E.U. market. And that's exactly what's happening. E.U. will have to legis-late to control companies in order to stabilize E.U. markets. E.U. is currently in a bind and the Euro is at the heart of the problems. Britain and Denmark were smart not to have joined; they have more variables to work with as a result. If Britain and Denmark are smart they can gain a distinctive market advantage over other European countries in the next couple of years.

The case of E.U. is important for showing that an integrated market has to be flexible enough for individual European markets to thrive. The Euro policy destroyed flexibility and harmed long-term economic growth for member countries.

As Europeans understood, China needs to understand that its neighbor markets are tied. But China must not make the same mistake of E.U. in legislating integration prematurely or making a unified currency. The E.U. may need a war to correct its downward spiral – or a miracle.

What China should do is recognize that Asian markets are linked and provide a collaborative possibility for Asian countries. ASEAN provides a positive forum for Asian countries to discuss problems and the needs of Asian countries. However, ASEAN has some fundamental and visible problems. First of all, ASEAN's economic unit is currently not capable of proposing a binding policy. China will have to provide leadership and cooperation to create a more viable structure for ASEAN so that it can make policies in times of crisis and implement them effectively.

Furthermore, China should provide a leading voice and an intellectual muscle so that ASEAN will be able to flex its muscle in the global market to benefit Asia. Unfortunately, ASEAN has been highly ineffective in this regard. Serious economic units, such as E.U., all but ignore ASEAN. G8 politely ignores anything that comes out of ASEAN. If Asian markets want to thrive in the 21st Century, this has to change. Asian markets' collective voice must command more global respect. It is when ASEAN can force larger economic bodies to consider Asian markets' needs, that individual Asian countries will be able to maintain a viable growth.

Economics, as ordered by Western Capitalism, is all about competition. Capitalism sees competition as fundamentally good. And Darwinism principle of the survival of the fittest is certainly a presumed value in Capitalist systems.

It is widely perceived globally that ASEAN is not fit to survive in the global market. No one would make such a claim for the E.U. While the E.U. is struggling from the weight of its recent integration, it is assumed that they will pick themselves up.

Perhaps, the perception is wrong. ASEAN is more fit to survive than it appears. But marketing principles in the west underscore the fact that even the negative perception is an indication of the weakness of ASEAN. Why is it that ASEAN cannot market itself effectively to have a better chip to bargain with in the global market?

Certainly, ASEAN needs to improve, and China can play a very important role. So far, all the indicators are there that China has not even begun to pay attention in this regard. China's lack of foresight will cost China in the long run. The Chinese market's success is tied more to Asia than it assumes. They are not in a Communist isolation any more. They have entered the global market. As much as China may profit from the global market, it is vulnerable to it, certainly more than when it was independent.

Besides intentionally playing a more involved role in existent pan-Asian institutions, China needs to invest in creating forums and think tanks to advance Asian economy. Having many think tanks is ideal because each think tank provides a different suggestion or idea for what is best at a given situation. With a diversity of suggestions, China and other Asian countries can have more informed options available to them.

The Chinese government will have to play an important role in creating think tanks specifically geared toward pan-Asian economics. First of all, the Chinese government should make a serious financial commitment in this regard. Secondly, China will have to hire a pan-Asian team of thinkers. There should be representative economics experts from many Asian countries. And they should be paid a very high salary to attract the best. Research done by these experts should be published in several Asian countries' languages and aggressively distributed throughout Asia. Fourthly, there should be a way for the findings to reach policy makers and translated into policy imple-mentation. There is currently no such agency that is effective or worthy of mention. Asia is filled with expert economists, but this human resource is not effectively managed or strategically structured to benefit China or Asia in the long run. In contrast, the West has dozens of effective and high profile think tanks dedicated to benefiting their client states or regions. In all probability, China will lose economic competition in the long run if something serious is not done.

China should heed Japan's example. Japan experienced economic boom and market leadership. However, its inability to create an effective think tank with consequences for the long-term economic growth of the Asian market is costing them. Japan is no longer so dominant economically. It is because of Japan's lack of foresight that Japan lost the possibility of being a market leader for the long-run. Now, Japan is heavily dependent on the US market for survival, so much more so than it ever was. It is important for a leading market to remain relatively independent. This is the only way that it is possible to maintain a long-term market leadership. For China to be able to survive as a thriving independent market, it must not forget that its independent market exists in the context of Asian economy. It is its closest and most real contextual relationship.

Besides integrating the Asian market for better structural support, China needs to create a viable internal financial structure. I use the word "create" because in my opinion there is no viable internal financial structure now in place in China to meet the changes in Chinese economy and the invasion of foreign markets which it has invited. China must learn from the failures of South Korea. The South Korean economy's near collapse could have single-handedly been prevented had the

Korean government paid more attention to its domestic financial infrastructure. While all aspects of the Korean economy grew, the Korean government did not update in light of the changes. It is a government's responsibility to oversee a type of domestic policy conducive to domestic economic viability.

The American government often uses the Federal Reserve to control interest rates and to prevent domestic economic failures. What the Federal Reserve Board does is dependent on a domestic financial infrastructure which is carefully investigated in research and modified in various controllable sectors as needs rise and in light of future forecasts that prompt preventive measures. No such active domestic policy and program exist in South Korea. The South Korean economy almost collapsed.

China is currently committing the same errors. While China will certainly see economic growth in dollar terms, it has no really serious policy to modify and direct its domestic financial institutions to meet the great changes that will come. Predictably, the failure to restructure its domestic financial infrastructure to handle the pressures and threats of global competition will compel China to lose the chess game in the global market.

In terms of creating a viable internal financial structure, I would make recommendations in these areas: (1) the Banking system and (2) Individual Property. These are fundamental to the Capitalist system in the West, and if China wants to continue to put itself into the global economy – structured from the Capitalist system – it must make modifications in its internal structure. Once you are in a system, you cannot control the impact of the outside on your economy, but you can strengthen your structure to meet the offensive.

First, China must make the Banking system more flexible. China must give its citizens greater access to its banks. Even though China is big, there has to be a type of modernization to benefit individual access to Chinese bank accounts on a national level. Just as an American bank customer from California can take out his cash via an ATM machine in Pennsylvania, a Chinese citizen in Shanghai with a Shanghai local bank account should be able to take out money in a bank in Mongolia.

This may seem like a simple suggestion, particularly for a Westerner, but China's banking system is inefficient. A small local bank in Shanghai does not allow account access at a small Mongolian bank. Being able to use ATMs nationally is more than accessing personal cash; it is related to the way banks cooperate and systems are harmonized. China has an overarching central system but not a very well-integrated national system. Even if all the banks were owned by the government, accessibility nationally is very limited as controls are localized. With the incursion of the Western market, this current inflexibility domestic-cally in China's banking will destroy it, potentially.

In order to update the Chinese Banking system, China will have to privatize some or all of its banks. There is no way that the Chinese government will be able to manage its banks efficiently as sweeping economic changes are forced upon China by its participation in the global market. If China did not want Western influences, then it should not have entered the global market in the first place. You can't just take Western money and allow Western firms into China without letting in Western intrusion in other areas. If China thought that it could do that, then obviously China needs to fire all of its current economic advisors and replace them with new ones.

And the Chinese Banking system must be privatized with very strict regulations to guard against corruption. As private corporations are allowed to compete for profit, they will have a vested interest in making the banking system efficient. The Chinese government can own banks and try to compete with private banks. This will show China a kind of market test of its own efficiency. I predict private banks will be much more efficient because of less bureaucracy and more directed attention. If limited privatization bears fruit after a few years, then China will know that it was the right way to go.

Details of privatization must be catered to the Chinese experience and in the first few years the government will have to actively encourage the growth of the private sector as well as guard it against corruption. China must do this as soon as possible since it has already entered the global market and is extremely vulnerable in the current inflexible state.

Another area of the Banking system that China will have to pay particular attention to is in the area of loans. The Chinese Banking system will have to develop a more efficient system for lending money to its citizens and those who want to start a small business. I understand that this goes fundamentally against the Chinese Stalinist-Marxist ideology. But China should have thought of that before choosing to participate in the global Capitalist system. China has betrayed Stalinist-Marxism by entering the global market. It has to bite the bullet and update its Banking system if it wants to survive.

Whereas when China was an isolationist Stalinist-Marxist state, there was hardly any way Capitalist systems could invade mainland China, now, just like a computer with no firewall is vulnerable to all kinds of manipulation from the outside, particularly by specialists, the Chinese market can be molded by outside Capitalists for their own gain to the detriment of Chinese citizens and China. Just like a computer user doesn't know generally that a bug or outside control mechanism has been placed inside his personal computer, China in current ignorance of the Capitalist system will not be able to detect many of the control mechanisms already in place inside China via western firms and agencies. Just as a computer can be manipulated without the owner's knowledge, China can be certain that the Western competition has already started to control Chinese markets from behind the scenes. Just as it will probably be too late for a personal computer user when he accidentally comes across the bug mechanism, if China leaves all to chance, China will only realize too late after most of its economy is, in fact, being controlled by outside mechanisms.

To prevent this, China must take active steps to reform its own Banking system so that it will be able to control it. It does seem like a contradiction to privatize, or give freedom, to the Chinese Banking system, in order to control it. But that's the fundamental principle in Capitalism. It's not surprising when one sees that Capitalism is built on Calvinistic principles. Calvinism states that God predestines and controls all action, but humans have complete free will. It's a paradox. And the Capitalist system has existed in such a paradox.

Giving freedom to the internal market in essence will give the government more access to controls. It is important that Chinese nationals be allowed to participate in the Chinese market and have vested interest in the growth of the Chinese market. In essence, such a policy is like training every citizen to be a soldier to fight Chinese economic wars. Some will be better soldiers than others. Some will play more important roles than others. Some only will be in the reserves. Some will only do desk duty or cooking service. But they will all be soldiers.

Updating the loan system helps efficiency and encourages individual citizen participation in the new Chinese market. It is crucial for individual citizens to be informed and grow together with Chinese corporations and the market, if China wants a sustained growth. China is the sum of its citizens.

There is no future for China without profit for its citizens. The Chinese government must pay more attention to its home and family than it is currently doing, trying to please foreign guests. In fact, ignoring the real needs of the current Chinese family – its citizens – goes against Confucianism, its history, and even the basic stress of Marxism.

The details of how the loan system is updated must be worked out by Chinese economists. They must, however, keep in mind that reforms must privilege greater access to loans for individual citizens and small companies. Emerging from a Communist system, this may actually be the biggest economic challenge for China. It's certainly far more difficult than creating structures needed to allow foreign companies into China. However, China's loan system (and Banking system) is far more important and must be the backbone of China's new economy.

The Banking system reform must be accompanied by greater access to private property. In fact, private property is crucial to any viable banking reform. I cannot stress enough the fact that China has to make concessions, such as allowing greater private property. It is understandable that it is difficult for a Stalinist-Marxist state like China to take the bold step and encourage private property. But I am confident that as a modernizing state, China, the heir to the Middle Kingdom, which boldly took the step of entering global markets, can take this difficult step. China was brave in turning its back on more outdated ideas that it had held to in order to survive and thrive in the global community, and China will have to take some steps domestically to ensure the success of its new bold policy.

Why is private property important in the Chinese context? Private property is crucial to the viability of China in the international market in the long run. No country has ever succeeded in a real, long-term sense without the participation of its citizens either directly or indirectly in the economic success. Currently, not allowing much access to private property is handicapping Chinese success in the long-run. Take for example, Russia. Russia was thrust into global economy without restrictions (unlike China) when Communism fell and Russia lost all control. The fact that citizens did not have private property was one of the biggest problems. Russia tried to implement a private property policy suddenly because they had no choice. The implementation was inefficient and certainly done without much thought or strategy. Thus, Russia was unable to capitalize on this important element for economic growth. Russia is still struggling with private property issues. It may not be wrong to argue that Russia's lack of foresight and planning regarding private property is one reason why Russia has been struggling to survive.

Of course, it is unlikely that Communism in China will suddenly fall. But it is possible. In fact, if China does not implement reforms, such as allowing greater property, Communism in China may fall sooner than later and push China into turmoil. China probably would prefer not to ex-perience a type of dam-breaking due to preventing private property unnecessarily.

It is in China's interest for growth and even survival to implement a more thought-out and systematically aggressive private property policy. Currently, China has the control of its domestic market. So this is actually the ideal time for China to take active steps to reform its own system.

There is a glimmer of hope in this regard. A few years back, China allowed access to privatization for some Chinese businesses. China understood that this was necessary if it were to open up its market to the West. It was a wise decision of the Chinese government. However, this decision has not been followed through adequately. There has not been a push to grant privatization to more local businesses. And certainly, privatization has not included active steps toward privatization of the citizenry.

It is understandable why it is difficult to encourage private property. China is a big country, and it would be a massive undertaking. There is also the question of implementation once a policy is outlined and passed into laws. But sooner China starts the process, the sooner China will be successful. China cannot afford to waste any more time.

China will have to focus on several areas for an effective implementation of its progressive economic policy. First of all, there has to be a think-tank dedicated to the endeavor. Perhaps, China can call this think thank, "Middle Kingdom Privatization Institute." But other names would suffice. The think tank does not have to be big. About 10 full-time scholars specializing in private property will be adequate. There should be representation from the field of private property law. Perhaps, China can locate a scholar in the West of Chinese descent who has studied private property law in the West. He can bring some insights on legal issues that affect the West. Western property law can be a type of a model to mold Chinese policy to meet Chinese needs.

There should also be a Chinese law scholar who deals with economy law and understands international law. This person should be a Chinese national and educated mostly in China. She can work together with the law scholar versed in Western property law. There should also be one sociologist whose research expertise is on popular interaction in China. Private property policies in the Chinese context will have to be done to maximize effective popular participation. Law scholars will have difficulty understanding popular needs as law education does not focus on that. Sociology, on the other hand, does, and so a sociologist will be a crucial part of the intellectual think tank. There should be one political science expert who understands the Chinese system as well. It would be helpful if China could actually locate a young scholar who assisted Chinese policy makers. The emphasis will be on his knowledge of the Chinese infrastructure, and this skill will provide important input on the implementation process at political structure levels. How can the policy be implemented at all political levels effectively to help China?

Other experts should include economists from Hong Kong. This is crucial because Hong Kong has extensive experiences with the West. As a part of China, Hong Kong has a vested interest in the long-term success of the Chinese economy. As such, Hong Kong's resident economists are ideal for providing important input. Rest of the economists should be from mainland China. China may want to invite some ethnic Chinese economists from other Asian countries, such as Singapore, Indonesia, and the Philippines. Certainly, their perspectives can help in formulating a viable economic structure of privatization for the Chinese context.

And the think tank should be in Beijing. It will be a government institution with the specific goal of helping the Chinese government implement a private property policy for China. Even though it will be a government institution that seeks the good of the Chinese government, the institute and the experts in the institute must be given freedom to investigate, research, and propose ideas with complete freedom of thought. Of course, the Chinese government can force all the researchers to keep discussions and ideas confidential. In fact, it would be good if China requires a security measure to protect information. Experts can discuss and propose ideas freely in the institute and make confidential document records. There is no reason why the outside world, or even the Chinese public, needs to know what is going on in the government think tank.

They can come up with 2-6 proposals in a confidential report on how China can implement a private property policy, and then it can be discussed in the financial divisions of the government and eventually implemented. As time is running out, the proposals should be made within 1-2 years. The government must decide on a course of action from the proposals within 3-6 months. Then, implementation must begin immediately according to plan. As China is thrust forward into the global economy, time is of the utmost importance. The inability to execute a plan in time can cost China billions of dollars in lost revenue and possibly its political stability as Western economic interests continue to reach deep into China.

When China allowed the West in, it allowed in Westerners who play by Western rules. They will try to manipulate the Chinese market. In fact, it is a part of Capitalism to do that. In the West, governments play a role in regulating sectors that can be harmful to national economic progress and encourage factors that can help economic progress. The factors are not constant. Sometimes, factors that help national economy this year may hurt national economy 10 years from now. In the fluidity of Western Capitalism, the government has to know what to do with each volatile change. This is why the West invests so heavily on economic think tanks. It's an issue of economic survival.

For China's economic survival, privatizing property must be a top priority for the Chinese government and its think tanks. This must be done in parallel to banking reforms. In fact, these two reforms will reinforce each other. For example, in the West procuring a bank loan requires commitment of private property. China will have to work through these issues (such as the relationship between private property and loans) as it tries to update its domestic economy for the 21st Century.

Another important program for China must be encouraging big businesses. It is not always a good idea to encourage big businesses. In fact, anti-trust laws of America and Europe have preserved healthy economic competition and encouraged economic growth. However, there are times that even Western countries turn a blind eye to violations of anti-trust laws. This is because big businesses are sometimes critical to national economic survival.

It would not be wrong to point out that the telephone system in the USA was a monopoly that helped USA when it needed the economic push. Eventually, the monopoly was broken up, but not before the monopoly served its purpose (from the US government's perspective) of helping US economy and society. Efficient telephone system helps businesses and economic transactions. It was because there was a monopoly that communication became very effective. In fact, when the telephone monopoly was broken up, America experienced a set-back. By then, however, American economy was strong enough to withstand the pressure.

China is not at a stage when unbridled competition will have a positive impact. Its economy has only recently entered capitalism and requires some protective measures. Encouraging big businesses is a type of a protectionist policy with the strategic goal of long-term economic growth. Eventually, China can be less encouraging of big businesses. In fact, China may even want to discourage big businesses in the future. But now is not the time for that. Now is the time for China to encourage big businesses. Big businesses can provide infrastructure building in key areas where the government normally cannot be as effective. Big businesses can thus function as pillars for the Chinese economy.

Besides the advantages that big businesses provide in terms of internal infrastructure building that accompany company expansion, big businesses can inject needed funds into the Chinese market and provide a greater fluidity of market transactions. This second advantage of big businesses is closely tied to the first. Big businesses need a more efficient infrastructure in terms of organization for production and for providing services more easily for consumers. But in order for big businesses to thrive and, in effect, pay for infrastructure building, they must find a way to (1) find a way to locate liquid funds that consumers can use to pay for products and services and (2) make business trans-actions (business to customer interactions) more efficient. In essence, as big businesses will need consumers to thrive and to make a profit, they will have a vested interest in seeing to making the consumer market more efficient. The very fact that awareness will be raised for the need for a more efficient internal market as big businesses expand will allow the Chinese government to gain key allies as it tries to reform Chinese economy to benefit China.

Furthermore, it is certain that big businesses themselves will take proactive steps to make the consumer more informed. This may take the form of sponsored public awareness campaigns by big businesses in terms of education courses (such as Microsoft courses on teaching Windows Excel programs) or aggressive advertisement. As more focus is geared toward making the Chinese public more informed consumers by helping them locate their market value and power, big businesses can play an important role in upgrading overall Chinese domestic economy and infrastructure.

Thirdly, supporting Chinese big businesses will provide a buffer against over-intrusion of foreign markets. China has to realize that most companies that enter China are billion-dollar corporations that exercise global influence and often have the implicit support of their government and political leaders. More often than not a multi-national corporation based in Germany, for instance, can count on Germany to pass favorable policy and legislation to help it expand internationally. Such a political push can also manifest itself in United Nations settings although it may be more clearly visible in economic contexts.

In other words, foreign companies entering the Chinese market have the implicit support of their countries in their dealings with the Chinese government and the Chinese market. As foreign companies are entering the Chinese market primarily for profit reasons, they will often not care what Chinese institutions are adversely affected in the process of their profit-taking. "It's business!" as the saying goes. The Chinese government can legislate to protect its populace, institutions, and economy, but such an in-your-face policy can adversely affect China's image and actually incur political and economic retaliation from foreign governing bodies that support their big businesses.

A better way for China to protect its people and market from a type of modern-day plundering of China is to think of global economics in terms of a Chess game. You don't always use the Queen to defend the King. Often, you use other pieces. You can consider big business as a significant chess piece that can play an important role in defending the King. The more competent big Chinese businesses are, they can actually buffer any attempt by foreign governments to gut the Chinese economy. For one, these Chinese businesses are in economic competition for profit as well. They know that the more foreign big businesses gut the market, less Chinese big businesses will take in terms of profit. Thus, in terms of profit taking alone, Chinese big businesses will provide a healthy competition and a type of buffer.

This buffer is particularly important because Chinese big businesses will be distinctively Chinese and almost all of its profits will go to China in one form or another. Most likely, these Chinese big businesses will use domestic resources and Chinese personnel, thereby directly impacting Chinese economic progress. Chinese businesses providing raw materials and needed services (business to business) will benefit and add to the overall growth of the Chinese economic progress.

It is important to emphasize that Chinese big businesses will use Chinese talent much more so than foreign businesses. Thus, effectively using human resources of China will make Chinese big businesses more suited to providing a healthy competitive wall so that domestic companies and Chinese people will have a long-term future. If a foreign company suddenly decides to leave China and relocate in Australia, for instance, Chinese managers probably will be fired. Foreign businesses have no real vested interest to seeing the good of the Chinese people. They are not a part of the Chinese society and are not bound by Chinese laws. Chinese big businesses are different. They are localized in the Chinese context, with Chinese social associations and political obligations. Chinese big businesses can be the biggest allies of the Chinese government even if they can't completely control them. Certainly, they can be indirect means to control foreign influences and intrusion into the Chinese market and society.

But perhaps the most important reason for encouraging big businesses is explained by a key concept in Reaganomics. President Ronald Reagan's administration emphasized the principle of "trickle-down economics." The fundamental principle in "trickle-down economics" is that is that if big businesses make big profits then the profits will filter down to every consumer. This makes a lot of sense. If there is more wealth generated, then the wealth will raise the standard of all Chinese people. Obviously, some people may experience a greater profit margin than others, but that is okay.

Some people work harder than others and probably deserve a greater profit margin. If big businesses make large profits, everyone wins eventually.

Consider how encouraging the growth of big businesses can help the working class directly. Let's just say, there is a Chinese electronic company and it is in the process of expanding. The Chinese government passes legislation helping the expansion of such companies and also grants tax breaks and other types of incentives, such as big low-interest loans. As a result, the Chinese electronics company gains a profit of 1 billion dollars. A large proportion of the profit will have to go to paying back loans and other types of investment accounts. And there needs to be funds set aside for future investments and development. Developments will most likely involve hiring more Chinese nationals. In essence, the success of a Chinese big business means creation of more jobs. More people will be employed and often with better pay.

Furthermore, as Chinese big businesses continue to make more and more money, it would be easier for China to pass legislation regarding the minimum wage. Chinese citizens will be working the same hours but will be paid more. This would be possible because Chinese big businesses will make large profits. If a big business is not willing to share its profits with its worker willingly as it would be ethical to do, China can step in and hold the big businesses up to their obligation to Chinese society and people. The important fact is that there is profit and money to go around so that such a legislation is even possible. If Chinese companies were not expanding and did not make large profits, then they would not have the money to hire new workers or pay existent workers more money.

Government incentives and support of big business expansion not only help big businesses, but also small businesses that big corporations depend on to provide needed business-to-business services and products as well as their workers and individual consumers. At this stage in Chinese economic progress, it is especially important to encourage big businesses. China has to focus on raising the general level of domestic economics and market structure. Equally important is the fact that China must encourage profit taking of Chinese corporations. There is a limit to how much a small company can make. However, bigger the company its ability to take large profits increases. By aggressively encouraging big businesses, general profit taking by all Chinese businesses will increase. China still needs a number of years to update and stabilize its domestic economic structure in lieu of opening up its market to the West. Encouraging Chinese big businesses will facilitate this process. It is true that there are possible complications, but they must be seen as the birth-pangs of a great economy in the 21st century.

Besides, China can handle the problems as they rise. What is important is that China does not remain a sitting giant which does not act when it needs to act. A lack of action can cost China. It is one thing to face and solve problems while moving forward and progressing, it is completely another things to have to solve problems in the process of retreat. Progress is important and is essential for the future. Retreat sounds the death knell.

All three elements are very important – reforming the Banking system, encouraging private property, and supporting big businesses. All these factors must be given immediate attention. All energy must be focused to make significant progresses in these areas. Inability to make the progress in these key sectors will create an economic disadvantage for China that can have a lasting impact.

CONCLUSION

China is on the verge of something great. There is no question about that. China can be one of the greatest nations in the world, a global power. Or China can lose its opportunity to make a mark in modern history as the global power. The choice is up to China.

China has taken necessary steps to enter the global competition. Obviously, if you are outside of the loop, you can't really compete for greatness. China now actively participates in the global competition. China has opened its arms to foreign investment. Foreign companies are invading the Chinese territory with a reckless abandon at China's request. Foreign investment capital is flowing in. Many foreign executives are flying in on their first class seats on American Airlines and Lufthansa. There is general optimism among Chinese officials. It seems like they can see the gold at the end of the rainbow.

But aggressive entry into global markets and the participation in the global economic competition have consequences. An isolationist country, like

China, may not be prepared to meet all the sweeping changes that are coming their way. Foreign investments and workers coming into the country mean changes. There will be social changes. There will be cultural changes. And there will be political changes.

In fact, playing by the rules of market Capitalism, Western companies and businesses are more than eager to tip the Chinese market to their advantage. Without taking some precautionary measures with a foresight, China can become a victim of modern day economic colonialism. China's resources can be plundered. China's wealth can be drained out of the country. The Chinese labor force can be used to the maximum benefit of Western companies, perhaps even with some amount of detrimental impact on Chinese citizens.

In these times, China must remember that it has an obligation to its citizens to put protective measures in place. China owes its long and illustrious history something more than passive responses to international corporate profit-taking. It would serve China well to think critically about the situation in light of its place in the global community and its historical experiences. It is important for China to ponder seriously about reform measures.

I have no doubt that China can succeed, if it puts its resources to reform itself in light of the present need and with an attention to the future. I have suggested key reforms needed in the areas of politics, education, and economics. I hope that China and its citizens will consider the proposed measures seriously. I am convinced that all of the proposed measures will help China tremendously and will ensure long-term economic success. Of course, I realize that China has its own set of values and expert opinions. I understand that it has a philosophy in all of the areas that I have discussed.

I do hope, however, that China will have an open-mind and consider the issues seriously. And I hope that after examining the issues carefully, China will choose a course that will be the best for itself and its populace.

But most importantly, whatever course China takes, I hope that China will have in view the common good of the human race. China can do a lot of good for the global human community. I hope that China will.

www.ingramcontent.com/pod-product-compliance
Lightning Source LLC
Chambersburg PA
CBHW020812300326
41914CB00075B/1687/J